DAILY PARENTING REFLECTIONS

A JOURNEY WITHIN

DAILY PARENTING REFLECTIONS

A JOURNEY WITHIN

R. Jill Maxwell

MAX ICEBREAKER LLC

Copyright © 2023 by Max Icebreaker, LLC
Print Edition

All rights reserved. No part of this publication may be reproduced, distributed, or transmitted in any form by any means, graphic, electronic, or mechanical, including photocopying, recording, taping, or stored in a database or retrieval system, without the prior written permission of the author or publisher except in the case of brief quotations embodied in critical articles and reviews.

Because of the dynamic nature of the Internet, any web addresses or links contained in this book may have changed since publication and may no longer be valid. The views expressed in this work are solely those of the author and do not necessarily reflect the views of the publisher, and the publisher hereby disclaims any responsibility for them.

ISBN: 978-1-7343831-2-6

DEDICATED TO ...

My mom, Joy, for triggering this journal's premise

My husband, Brandon, for being my partner in this parenting thing

Our three amazing offspring Jessica, Alexandra, and Jack for "raising" me

All parents who want to grow and show up as the best version of themselves

DAILY PARENTING REFLECTIONS

A JOURNEY WITHIN

DAILY PARENTING REFLECTIONS

How to Use This Journal

WHETHER YOU'RE A PARENT-TO-BE, a parent of one, or a team, this journal is for **YOU**! This is **not** about your child's milestones (although what you write may coincide with a few). This journal is YOUR safe space to be honest with you. Feel free to get your co-parent one!

The goal of these pages is to get to KNOW THYSELF, appreciate who and where you are in your life, and, through your children's behaviors reflected at you like mirrors, admit where you need to grow. This journal may serve as a pat on the back on those days when you feel you got it right. Write that down! On those "needs improvement" days (we ALL have them – children are humbling), recognize those moments, too. Like the time our two-and-a-half-year-old decided to teach us the finer points of road rage vocabulary and yelled, "ATHHOLE!" from the backseat of our car with perfect timing. My husband and I looked at each other and agreed lesson learned! Toddlers and road etiquette don't mix. Kids are always listening, learning, mimicking, and watching us. Preteens and teens, too!

You see, and this is tricky to accept, we don't raise and teach our kids. *WISDOM ALERT* Our children come here to mirror to us who WE are. WHOA! Who knew parenting was a crash course in self-discovery? Certainly not us when our biggest concern was picking out the perfect baby name – little did we know they were picking ours.

My husband and I have brought up three amazing children, but we could have used a manual or cheat sheet to help us. That's what this journal will provide. The childrearing stage of life flies! Faster than you can say, "I swear they were just in diapers yesterday." And, just like children, our world now is changing fast. The entire planet is evolving, so it's in your (and your family's) best interest to evolve, too.

My mom reminded me of how much she has learned from my siblings and me over the years. "Parents have to be _open_ to wanting to learn from their children," she said. "Took me years to learn, but you were open to learning from yours from the start." It was in wanting to help my own, and this generation of children at large, that triggered this journal.

The parenting trip is filled with joy and fear, highs and lows, good days and horrible ones, but always with love. The parenting role shifts once you *realize* that our children consistently show us who we are (impatient, easily agitated, funny, loving, gentle, Neanderthal-like, etc.). Children teach us that if we are controlling, they may control in return through sass and whining, for example. If we are needy, they reject us or drown us with clinginess. If we are frustrated, impatient, and/or yelling, they'll yell at the family pet or throw things.

You'll write down in this journal how you appreciated (or didn't) seeing that behavior in your child. Either way, if they are expressing it, you just might be, too. Ask yourself what you need to become more aware of in YOU to be a better role model. The prompts on the following pages will assist you in your awareness.

REMEMBER! Just as we all have gifts and talents we acquired from our parents (birth or adopted), we also have some less-than-glowing ones. <u>Your</u> children have a combination of them also from <u>you</u>! Don't be so hard on yourself or your significant other. No blaming. The objective here is to learn how to HELP yourself grow into the parent you want to be. **When you change, everything around you changes, including, and especially, your children.**

Another goal of this journal is to keep memories alive that you don't want to lose. In the blur of middle-of-the-night feedings, wondering if the little darlings will ever use a toilet, and surviving middle school cafeteria angst, it's easy to forget the striking moment of recognition from those riveted eyes or the grace of your tolerant family pet's ear grabbed like a lifeline. All those moments and how YOU react will be recorded in your child's soul and can be encouraged or corrected through trial and error. Forgive yourself when disrespect or name-calling appears, for example, and get better each time. It is <u>not</u> incumbent upon the child to change. It is crucial for YOU to adjust and grow! They will follow your lead.

Each day will be a marvel of lessons between you and your offspring, so BE OPEN!

The format is simple. Fill in the date and your child's age. Answer each question, then jot down your thoughts *in this journal*. A few sentences, keywords, bullet points, YOU decide. No rules except one: **BE HONEST** with <u>yourself</u>. No BS. Everything children learn, they learn from you, so remember to return patient energy to yourself. No blaming or shaming. Speaking of honesty, some days this journal will be all you can do to find clarity, or you might miss more than a few...days. Be as diligent as possible. Just pick up where you left off. This is to help <u>you</u> see <u>you</u>.

Please remember that this journal is about YOUR growth!!! When you grow, you will be a better example for your child, your marriage will grow, family and friend relationships will go smoother, and, MOST importantly, YOU will appreciate _you_ more! Everyone in your world benefits from your growth. I repeat: when you change, everything around you changes.

PLEASE remember that there is NOTHING wrong with you! We all have human moments overflowing with gifts and shortcomings. The goal here isn't to be the "perfect" parent. Be who you are, not who everyone else tells you to be. Seek the best version of your loving, forgiving, courageous, understanding, joyful self. YOU'RE OKAY!

Be brave! Let's dig in and discover what your child taught you about yourself today!

TODAY'S DATE _____

CHILD'S NAME/AGE _____

_____

1. What behavior did my child exhibit today that caught my attention?

_____

_____

2. Do I want my child to keep it? Is it in my child's greatest interest?

_____

_____

3. Did watching that trait make me laugh and smile?

_____

_____

4. Did the behavior trigger me? What would I like my child to exhibit instead?

_____

_____

To know thyself is the beginning of wisdom.

Socrates

5. Do I even see the behavior in myself? Am I willing to change or alter the same behavior in me?

_____

_____

6. What change do I need to make in myself to be a better role model, so my young one will exhibit **that** behavior instead?

_____

_____

_____

7. Time to take a moment to reflect on what I've learned about myself from my child. Jot down a few thoughts (i.e., wishes, hopes, courageousness, forgiveness, acceptance, encouragement, etc...) about me. What plan will I make to improve myself and become my child's best example?

_____

_____

_____

_____

TODAY'S DATE _____

CHILD'S NAME/AGE _____

_____

1. What behavior did my child exhibit today that caught my attention?

   _____

   _____

2. Do I want my child to keep it? Is it in my child's greatest interest?

   _____

   _____

3. Did watching that trait make me laugh and smile?

   _____

   _____

4. Did the behavior trigger me? What would I like my child to exhibit instead?

   _____

   _____

To know thyself is the beginning of wisdom.

Socrates

5. Do I even see the behavior in myself? Am I willing to change or alter the same behavior in me?

_____
_____

6. What change do I need to make in myself to be a better role model, so my young one will exhibit **that** behavior instead?

_____
_____
_____

7. Time to take a moment to reflect on what I've learned about myself from my child. Jot down a few thoughts (i.e., wishes, hopes, courageousness, forgiveness, acceptance, encouragement, etc...) about me. What plan will I make to improve myself and become my child's best example?

_____
_____
_____
_____

TODAY'S DATE _____

CHILD'S NAME/AGE _____

_____

1. What behavior did my child exhibit today that caught my attention?

   _____

   _____

2. Do I want my child to keep it? Is it in my child's greatest interest?

   _____

   _____

3. Did watching that trait make me laugh and smile?

   _____

   _____

4. Did the behavior trigger me? What would I like my child to exhibit instead?

   _____

   _____

> To know thyself is the beginning of wisdom.
> Socrates

5. Do I even see the behavior in myself? Am I willing to change or alter the same behavior in me?

_____
_____

6. What change do I need to make in myself to be a better role model, so my young one will exhibit **that** behavior instead?

_____
_____
_____

7. Time to take a moment to reflect on what I've learned about myself from my child. Jot down a few thoughts (i.e., wishes, hopes, courageousness, forgiveness, acceptance, encouragement, etc…) about me. What plan will I make to improve myself and become my child's best example?

_____
_____
_____
_____

TODAY'S DATE _____

CHILD'S NAME/AGE _____

_____

1. What behavior did my child exhibit today that caught my attention?

   _____

   _____

2. Do I want my child to keep it? Is it in my child's greatest interest?

   _____

   _____

3. Did watching that trait make me laugh and smile?

   _____

   _____

4. Did the behavior trigger me? What would I like my child to exhibit instead?

   _____

   _____

To know thyself is the beginning of wisdom.

Socrates

DAILY PARENTING REFLECTIONS

5. Do I even see the behavior in myself? Am I willing to change or alter the same behavior in me?

_____

_____

6. What change do I need to make in myself to be a better role model, so my young one will exhibit **that** behavior instead?

_____

_____

_____

7. Time to take a moment to reflect on what I've learned about myself from my child. Jot down a few thoughts (i.e., wishes, hopes, courageousness, forgiveness, acceptance, encouragement, etc...) about me. What plan will I make to improve myself and become my child's best example?

_____

_____

_____

_____

TODAY'S DATE _____

CHILD'S NAME/AGE _____

_____

1. What behavior did my child exhibit today that caught my attention?

   _____
   _____

2. Do I want my child to keep it? Is it in my child's greatest interest?

   _____
   _____

3. Did watching that trait make me laugh and smile?

   _____
   _____

4. Did the behavior trigger me? What would I like my child to exhibit instead?

   _____
   _____

> To know thyself is the beginning of wisdom.
> Socrates

5. Do I even see the behavior in myself? Am I willing to change or alter the same behavior in me?

6. What change do I need to make in myself to be a better role model, so my young one will exhibit **that** behavior instead?

7. Time to take a moment to reflect on what I've learned about myself from my child. Jot down a few thoughts (i.e., wishes, hopes, courageousness, forgiveness, acceptance, encouragement, etc…) about me. What plan will I make to improve myself and become my child's best example?

TODAY'S DATE _____

CHILD'S NAME/AGE _____

_____

1. What behavior did my child exhibit today that caught my attention?

   _____

   _____

2. Do I want my child to keep it? Is it in my child's greatest interest?

   _____

   _____

3. Did watching that trait make me laugh and smile?

   _____

   _____

4. Did the behavior trigger me? What would I like my child to exhibit instead?

   _____

   _____

> To know thyself is the beginning of wisdom.
> Socrates

5. Do I even see the behavior in myself? Am I willing to change or alter the same behavior in me?

_____

_____

6. What change do I need to make in myself to be a better role model, so my young one will exhibit **that** behavior instead?

_____

_____

_____

7. Time to take a moment to reflect on what I've learned about myself from my child. Jot down a few thoughts (i.e., wishes, hopes, courageousness, forgiveness, acceptance, encouragement, etc…) about me. What plan will I make to improve myself and become my child's best example?

_____

_____

_____

_____

TODAY'S DATE _____

CHILD'S NAME/AGE _____

_____

1. What behavior did my child exhibit today that caught my attention?

   _____

   _____

2. Do I want my child to keep it? Is it in my child's greatest interest?

   _____

   _____

3. Did watching that trait make me laugh and smile?

   _____

   _____

4. Did the behavior trigger me? What would I like my child to exhibit instead?

   _____

   _____

To know thyself is the beginning of wisdom.
Socrates

5. Do I even see the behavior in myself? Am I willing to change or alter the same behavior in me?

_____
_____

6. What change do I need to make in myself to be a better role model, so my young one will exhibit **that** behavior instead?

_____
_____
_____

7. Time to take a moment to reflect on what I've learned about myself from my child. Jot down a few thoughts (i.e., wishes, hopes, courageousness, forgiveness, acceptance, encouragement, etc…) about me. What plan will I make to improve myself and become my child's best example?

_____
_____
_____
_____

TODAY'S DATE _____

CHILD'S NAME/AGE _____

_____

1. What behavior did my child exhibit today that caught my attention?

   _____

   _____

2. Do I want my child to keep it? Is it in my child's greatest interest?

   _____

   _____

3. Did watching that trait make me laugh and smile?

   _____

   _____

4. Did the behavior trigger me? What would I like my child to exhibit instead?

   _____

   _____

To know thyself is the beginning of wisdom.
Socrates

DAILY PARENTING REFLECTIONS

5. Do I even see the behavior in myself? Am I willing to change or alter the same behavior in me?

_____

_____

6. What change do I need to make in myself to be a better role model, so my young one will exhibit **that** behavior instead?

_____

_____

_____

7. Time to take a moment to reflect on what I've learned about myself from my child. Jot down a few thoughts (i.e., wishes, hopes, courageousness, forgiveness, acceptance, encouragement, etc…) about me. What plan will I make to improve myself and become my child's best example?

_____

_____

_____

_____

TODAY'S DATE _____

CHILD'S NAME/AGE _____

_____

1. What behavior did my child exhibit today that caught my attention?

   _____
   _____

2. Do I want my child to keep it? Is it in my child's greatest interest?

   _____
   _____

3. Did watching that trait make me laugh and smile?

   _____
   _____

4. Did the behavior trigger me? What would I like my child to exhibit instead?

   _____
   _____

To know thyself is the beginning of wisdom.
Socrates

5. Do I even see the behavior in myself? Am I willing to change or alter the same behavior in me?

_____

_____

6. What change do I need to make in myself to be a better role model, so my young one will exhibit **that** behavior instead?

_____

_____

_____

7. Time to take a moment to reflect on what I've learned about myself from my child. Jot down a few thoughts (i.e., wishes, hopes, courageousness, forgiveness, acceptance, encouragement, etc...) about me. What plan will I make to improve myself and become my child's best example?

_____

_____

_____

_____

_____

TODAY'S DATE _____

CHILD'S NAME/AGE _____

_____

1. What behavior did my child exhibit today that caught my attention?

   _____

   _____

2. Do I want my child to keep it? Is it in my child's greatest interest?

   _____

   _____

3. Did watching that trait make me laugh and smile?

   _____

   _____

4. Did the behavior trigger me? What would I like my child to exhibit instead?

   _____

   _____

To know thyself is the beginning of wisdom.
Socrates

DAILY PARENTING REFLECTIONS

5. Do I even see the behavior in myself? Am I willing to change or alter the same behavior in me?

_____

_____

6. What change do I need to make in myself to be a better role model, so my young one will exhibit **that** behavior instead?

_____

_____

7. Time to take a moment to reflect on what I've learned about myself from my child. Jot down a few thoughts (i.e., wishes, hopes, courageousness, forgiveness, acceptance, encouragement, etc...) about me. What plan will I make to improve myself and become my child's best example?

_____

_____

_____

_____

TODAY'S DATE _____

CHILD'S NAME/AGE _____

_____

1. What behavior did my child exhibit today that caught my attention?

   _____

   _____

2. Do I want my child to keep it? Is it in my child's greatest interest?

   _____

   _____

3. Did watching that trait make me laugh and smile?

   _____

   _____

4. Did the behavior trigger me? What would I like my child to exhibit instead?

   _____

   _____

To know thyself is the beginning of wisdom.
Socrates

5. Do I even see the behavior in myself? Am I willing to change or alter the same behavior in me?

_____

_____

6. What change do I need to make in myself to be a better role model, so my young one will exhibit **that** behavior instead?

_____

_____

7. Time to take a moment to reflect on what I've learned about myself from my child. Jot down a few thoughts (i.e., wishes, hopes, courageousness, forgiveness, acceptance, encouragement, etc...) about me. What plan will I make to improve myself and become my child's best example?

_____

_____

_____

_____

TODAY'S DATE _____

CHILD'S NAME/AGE _____

_____

1. What behavior did my child exhibit today that caught my attention?

   _____

   _____

2. Do I want my child to keep it? Is it in my child's greatest interest?

   _____

   _____

3. Did watching that trait make me laugh and smile?

   _____

   _____

4. Did the behavior trigger me? What would I like my child to exhibit instead?

   _____

   _____

To know thyself is the beginning of wisdom.

Socrates

5. Do I even see the behavior in myself? Am I willing to change or alter the same behavior in me?

_____
_____

6. What change do I need to make in myself to be a better role model, so my young one will exhibit **that** behavior instead?

_____
_____
_____

7. Time to take a moment to reflect on what I've learned about myself from my child. Jot down a few thoughts (i.e., wishes, hopes, courageousness, forgiveness, acceptance, encouragement, etc...) about me. What plan will I make to improve myself and become my child's best example?

_____
_____
_____
_____

TODAY'S DATE _____

CHILD'S NAME/AGE _____

_____

1. What behavior did my child exhibit today that caught my attention?

_____

_____

2. Do I want my child to keep it? Is it in my child's greatest interest?

_____

_____

3. Did watching that trait make me laugh and smile?

_____

_____

4. Did the behavior trigger me? What would I like my child to exhibit instead?

_____

_____

To know thyself is the beginning of wisdom.
Socrates

5. Do I even see the behavior in myself? Am I willing to change or alter the same behavior in me?

_____
_____

6. What change do I need to make in myself to be a better role model, so my young one will exhibit **that** behavior instead?

_____
_____
_____

7. Time to take a moment to reflect on what I've learned about myself from my child. Jot down a few thoughts (i.e., wishes, hopes, courageousness, forgiveness, acceptance, encouragement, etc...) about me. What plan will I make to improve myself and become my child's best example?

_____
_____
_____
_____

TODAY'S DATE _____

CHILD'S NAME/AGE _____

_____

1. What behavior did my child exhibit today that caught my attention?

   _____

   _____

2. Do I want my child to keep it? Is it in my child's greatest interest?

   _____

   _____

3. Did watching that trait make me laugh and smile?

   _____

   _____

4. Did the behavior trigger me? What would I like my child to exhibit instead?

   _____

   _____

To know thyself is the beginning of wisdom.
Socrates

5. Do I even see the behavior in myself? Am I willing to change or alter the same behavior in me?

_____
_____

6. What change do I need to make in myself to be a better role model, so my young one will exhibit **that** behavior instead?

_____
_____
_____

7. Time to take a moment to reflect on what I've learned about myself from my child. Jot down a few thoughts (i.e., wishes, hopes, courageousness, forgiveness, acceptance, encouragement, etc…) about me. What plan will I make to improve myself and become my child's best example?

_____
_____
_____
_____

TODAY'S DATE _____

CHILD'S NAME/AGE _____

_____

1. What behavior did my child exhibit today that caught my attention?

   _____

   _____

2. Do I want my child to keep it? Is it in my child's greatest interest?

   _____

   _____

3. Did watching that trait make me laugh and smile?

   _____

   _____

4. Did the behavior trigger me? What would I like my child to exhibit instead?

   _____

   _____

To know thyself is the beginning of wisdom.
Socrates

5. Do I even see the behavior in myself? Am I willing to change or alter the same behavior in me?

_____

_____

6. What change do I need to make in myself to be a better role model, so my young one will exhibit **that** behavior instead?

_____

_____

_____

7. Time to take a moment to reflect on what I've learned about myself from my child. Jot down a few thoughts (i.e., wishes, hopes, courageousness, forgiveness, acceptance, encouragement, etc...) about me. What plan will I make to improve myself and become my child's best example?

_____

_____

_____

_____

TODAY'S DATE _____

CHILD'S NAME/AGE _____

_____

1. What behavior did my child exhibit today that caught my attention?

   _____
   _____

2. Do I want my child to keep it? Is it in my child's greatest interest?

   _____
   _____

3. Did watching that trait make me laugh and smile?

   _____
   _____

4. Did the behavior trigger me? What would I like my child to exhibit instead?

   _____
   _____

> To know thyself is the beginning of wisdom.
> Socrates

5. Do I even see the behavior in myself? Am I willing to change or alter the same behavior in me?

_____

_____

6. What change do I need to make in myself to be a better role model, so my young one will exhibit **that** behavior instead?

_____

_____

_____

7. Time to take a moment to reflect on what I've learned about myself from my child. Jot down a few thoughts (i.e., wishes, hopes, courageousness, forgiveness, acceptance, encouragement, etc...) about me. What plan will I make to improve myself and become my child's best example?

_____

_____

_____

_____

TODAY'S DATE _____

CHILD'S NAME/AGE _____

_____

1. What behavior did my child exhibit today that caught my attention?

   _____
   _____

2. Do I want my child to keep it? Is it in my child's greatest interest?

   _____
   _____

3. Did watching that trait make me laugh and smile?

   _____
   _____

4. Did the behavior trigger me? What would I like my child to exhibit instead?

   _____
   _____

> To know thyself is the beginning of wisdom.
> Socrates

DAILY PARENTING REFLECTIONS

5. Do I even see the behavior in myself? Am I willing to change or alter the same behavior in me?

_____

_____

6. What change do I need to make in myself to be a better role model, so my young one will exhibit **that** behavior instead?

_____

_____

_____

7. Time to take a moment to reflect on what I've learned about myself from my child. Jot down a few thoughts (i.e., wishes, hopes, courageousness, forgiveness, acceptance, encouragement, etc...) about me. What plan will I make to improve myself and become my child's best example?

_____

_____

_____

_____

TODAY'S DATE _____

CHILD'S NAME/AGE _____

_____

1. What behavior did my child exhibit today that caught my attention?

   _____

   _____

2. Do I want my child to keep it? Is it in my child's greatest interest?

   _____

   _____

3. Did watching that trait make me laugh and smile?

   _____

   _____

4. Did the behavior trigger me? What would I like my child to exhibit instead?

   _____

   _____

TO KNOW THYSELF IS THE BEGINNING OF WISDOM.
SOCRATES

5. Do I even see the behavior in myself? Am I willing to change or alter the same behavior in me?

_____
_____

6. What change do I need to make in myself to be a better role model, so my young one will exhibit **that** behavior instead?

_____
_____
_____

7. Time to take a moment to reflect on what I've learned about myself from my child. Jot down a few thoughts (i.e., wishes, hopes, courageousness, forgiveness, acceptance, encouragement, etc...) about me. What plan will I make to improve myself and become my child's best example?

_____
_____
_____
_____

TODAY'S DATE _____

CHILD'S NAME/AGE _____

_____

1. What behavior did my child exhibit today that caught my attention?

   _____

   _____

2. Do I want my child to keep it? Is it in my child's greatest interest?

   _____

   _____

3. Did watching that trait make me laugh and smile?

   _____

   _____

4. Did the behavior trigger me? What would i like my child to exhibit instead?

   _____

   _____

To know thyself is the beginning of wisdom.
Socrates

5. Do I even see the behavior in myself? Am I willing to change or alter the same behavior in me?

_____

_____

6. What change do I need to make in myself to be a better role model, so my young one will exhibit **that** behavior instead?

_____

_____

_____

7. Time to take a moment to reflect on what I've learned about myself from my child. Jot down a few thoughts (i.e., wishes, hopes, courageousness, forgiveness, acceptance, encouragement, etc…) about me. What plan will I make to improve myself and become my child's best example?

_____

_____

_____

_____

TODAY'S DATE _____

CHILD'S NAME/AGE _____

_____

1. What behavior did my child exhibit today that caught my attention?

   _____

   _____

2. Do I want my child to keep it? Is it in my child's greatest interest?

   _____

   _____

3. Did watching that trait make me laugh and smile?

   _____

   _____

4. Did the behavior trigger me? What would I like my child to exhibit instead?

   _____

   _____

To know thyself is the beginning of wisdom.
Socrates

5. Do I even see the behavior in myself? Am I willing to change or alter the same behavior in me?

6. What change do I need to make in myself to be a better role model, so my young one will exhibit **that** behavior instead?

7. Time to take a moment to reflect on what I've learned about myself from my child. Jot down a few thoughts (i.e., wishes, hopes, courageousness, forgiveness, acceptance, encouragement, etc…) about me. What plan will I make to improve myself and become my child's best example?

TODAY'S DATE _____

CHILD'S NAME/AGE _____

_____

1. What behavior did my child exhibit today that caught my attention?

_____

_____

2. Do I want my child to keep it? Is it in my child's greatest interest?

_____

_____

3. Did watching that trait make me laugh and smile?

_____

_____

4. Did the behavior trigger me? What would I like my child to exhibit instead?

_____

_____

To know thyself is the beginning of wisdom.
Socrates

5. Do I even see the behavior in myself? Am I willing to change or alter the same behavior in me?

_____

_____

6. What change do I need to make in myself to be a better role model, so my young one will exhibit **that** behavior instead?

_____

_____

_____

7. Time to take a moment to reflect on what I've learned about myself from my child. Jot down a few thoughts (i.e., wishes, hopes, courageousness, forgiveness, acceptance, encouragement, etc...) about me. What plan will I make to improve myself and become my child's best example?

_____

_____

_____

_____

TODAY'S DATE _____

CHILD'S NAME/AGE _____

_____

1. What behavior did my child exhibit today that caught my attention?

   _____
   _____

2. Do I want my child to keep it? Is it in my child's greatest interest?

   _____
   _____

3. Did watching that trait make me laugh and smile?

   _____
   _____

4. Did the behavior trigger me? What would I like my child to exhibit instead?

   _____
   _____

To know thyself is the beginning of wisdom.
Socrates

5. Do I even see the behavior in myself? Am I willing to change or alter the same behavior in me?

_____

_____

6. What change do I need to make in myself to be a better role model, so my young one will exhibit **that** behavior instead?

_____

_____

7. Time to take a moment to reflect on what I've learned about myself from my child. Jot down a few thoughts (i.e., wishes, hopes, courageousness, forgiveness, acceptance, encouragement, etc…) about me. What plan will I make to improve myself and become my child's best example?

_____

_____

_____

_____

TODAY'S DATE _____

CHILD'S NAME/AGE _____

_____

1. What behavior did my child exhibit today that caught my attention?

   _____

   _____

2. Do I want my child to keep it? Is it in my child's greatest interest?

   _____

   _____

3. Did watching that trait make me laugh and smile?

   _____

   _____

4. Did the behavior trigger me? What would I like my child to exhibit instead?

   _____

   _____

To know thyself is the beginning of wisdom.
Socrates

5. Do I even see the behavior in myself? Am I willing to change or alter the same behavior in me?

_____

_____

6. What change do I need to make in myself to be a better role model, so my young one will exhibit **that** behavior instead?

_____

_____

_____

7. Time to take a moment to reflect on what I've learned about myself from my child. Jot down a few thoughts (i.e., wishes, hopes, courageousness, forgiveness, acceptance, encouragement, etc...) about me. What plan will I make to improve myself and become my child's best example?

_____

_____

_____

_____

TODAY'S DATE _____

CHILD'S NAME/AGE _____

_____

1. What behavior did my child exhibit today that caught my attention?

   _____

   _____

2. Do I want my child to keep it? Is it in my child's greatest interest?

   _____

   _____

3. Did watching that trait make me laugh and smile?

   _____

   _____

4. Did the behavior trigger me? What would I like my child to exhibit instead?

   _____

   _____

To know thyself is the beginning of wisdom.

Socrates

5. Do I even see the behavior in myself? Am I willing to change or alter the same behavior in me?

6. What change do I need to make in myself to be a better role model, so my young one will exhibit **that** behavior instead?

7. Time to take a moment to reflect on what I've learned about myself from my child. Jot down a few thoughts (i.e., wishes, hopes, courageousness, forgiveness, acceptance, encouragement, etc...) about me. What plan will I make to improve myself and become my child's best example?

TODAY'S DATE _____

CHILD'S NAME/AGE _____

_____

1. What behavior did my child exhibit today that caught my attention?

   _____
   _____

2. Do I want my child to keep it? Is it in my child's greatest interest?

   _____
   _____

3. Did watching that trait make me laugh and smile?

   _____
   _____

4. Did the behavior trigger me? What would I like my child to exhibit instead?

   _____
   _____

To know thyself is the beginning of wisdom.
Socrates

5. Do I even see the behavior in myself? Am I willing to change or alter the same behavior in me?

6. What change do I need to make in myself to be a better role model, so my young one will exhibit **that** behavior instead?

7. Time to take a moment to reflect on what I've learned about myself from my child. Jot down a few thoughts (i.e., wishes, hopes, courageousness, forgiveness, acceptance, encouragement, etc...) about me. What plan will I make to improve myself and become my child's best example?

TODAY'S DATE _____

CHILD'S NAME/AGE _____

_____

1. What behavior did my child exhibit today that caught my attention?

_____

_____

2. Do I want my child to keep it? Is it in my child's greatest interest?

_____

_____

3. Did watching that trait make me laugh and smile?

_____

_____

4. Did the behavior trigger me? What would I like my child to exhibit instead?

_____

_____

To know thyself is the beginning of wisdom.

Socrates

5. Do I even see the behavior in myself? Am I willing to change or alter the same behavior in me?

_____
_____

6. What change do I need to make in myself to be a better role model, so my young one will exhibit **that** behavior instead?

_____
_____
_____

7. Time to take a moment to reflect on what I've learned about myself from my child. Jot down a few thoughts (i.e., wishes, hopes, courageousness, forgiveness, acceptance, encouragement, etc…) about me. What plan will I make to improve myself and become my child's best example?

_____
_____
_____
_____

TODAY'S DATE _____

CHILD'S NAME/AGE _____

_____

1. What behavior did my child exhibit today that caught my attention?

   _____
   _____

2. Do I want my child to keep it? Is it in my child's greatest interest?

   _____
   _____

3. Did watching that trait make me laugh and smile?

   _____
   _____

4. Did the behavior trigger me? What would I like my child to exhibit instead?

   _____
   _____

To know thyself is the beginning of wisdom.
Socrates

5. Do I even see the behavior in myself? Am I willing to change or alter the same behavior in me?

6. What change do I need to make in myself to be a better role model, so my young one will exhibit **that** behavior instead?

7. Time to take a moment to reflect on what I've learned about myself from my child. Jot down a few thoughts (i.e., wishes, hopes, courageousness, forgiveness, acceptance, encouragement, etc…) about me. What plan will I make to improve myself and become my child's best example?

TODAY'S DATE _____

CHILD'S NAME/AGE _____

_____

1. What behavior did my child exhibit today that caught my attention?

   _____
   _____

2. Do I want my child to keep it? Is it in my child's greatest interest?

   _____
   _____

3. Did watching that trait make me laugh and smile?

   _____
   _____

4. Did the behavior trigger me? What would I like my child to exhibit instead?

   _____
   _____

To know thyself is the beginning of wisdom.
Socrates

5. Do I even see the behavior in myself? Am I willing to change or alter the same behavior in me?

6. What change do I need to make in myself to be a better role model, so my young one will exhibit **that** behavior instead?

7. Time to take a moment to reflect on what I've learned about myself from my child. Jot down a few thoughts (i.e., wishes, hopes, courageousness, forgiveness, acceptance, encouragement, etc...) about me. What plan will I make to improve myself and become my child's best example?

TODAY'S DATE _____

CHILD'S NAME/AGE _____

_____

1. What behavior did my child exhibit today that caught my attention?

   _____

   _____

2. Do I want my child to keep it? Is it in my child's greatest interest?

   _____

   _____

3. Did watching that trait make me laugh and smile?

   _____

   _____

4. Did the behavior trigger me? What would I like my child to exhibit instead?

   _____

   _____

To know thyself is the beginning of wisdom.

Socrates

5. Do I even see the behavior in myself? Am I willing to change or alter the same behavior in me?

6. What change do I need to make in myself to be a better role model, so my young one will exhibit **that** behavior instead?

7. Time to take a moment to reflect on what I've learned about myself from my child. Jot down a few thoughts (i.e., wishes, hopes, courageousness, forgiveness, acceptance, encouragement, etc…) about me. What plan will I make to improve myself and become my child's best example?

TODAY'S DATE _____

CHILD'S NAME/AGE _____

_____

1. What behavior did my child exhibit today that caught my attention?

   _____
   _____

2. Do I want my child to keep it? Is it in my child's greatest interest?

   _____
   _____

3. Did watching that trait make me laugh and smile?

   _____
   _____

4. Did the behavior trigger me? What would I like my child to exhibit instead?

   _____
   _____

To know thyself is the beginning of wisdom.
Socrates

5. Do I even see the behavior in myself? Am I willing to change or alter the same behavior in me?

6. What change do I need to make in myself to be a better role model, so my young one will exhibit **that** behavior instead?

7. Time to take a moment to reflect on what I've learned about myself from my child. Jot down a few thoughts (i.e., wishes, hopes, courageousness, forgiveness, acceptance, encouragement, etc…) about me. What plan will I make to improve myself and become my child's best example?

TODAY'S DATE _____

CHILD'S NAME/AGE _____

_____

1. What behavior did my child exhibit today that caught my attention?

   _____

   _____

2. Do I want my child to keep it? Is it in my child's greatest interest?

   _____

   _____

3. Did watching that trait make me laugh and smile?

   _____

   _____

4. Did the behavior trigger me? What would I like my child to exhibit instead?

   _____

   _____

To know thyself is the beginning of wisdom.
Socrates

5. Do I even see the behavior in myself? Am I willing to change or alter the same behavior in me?

_____

_____

6. What change do I need to make in myself to be a better role model, so my young one will exhibit **that** behavior instead?

_____

_____

_____

7. Time to take a moment to reflect on what I've learned about myself from my child. Jot down a few thoughts (i.e., wishes, hopes, courageousness, forgiveness, acceptance, encouragement, etc...) about me. What plan will I make to improve myself and become my child's best example?

_____

_____

_____

_____

TODAY'S DATE _____

CHILD'S NAME/AGE _____

_____

1. What behavior did my child exhibit today that caught my attention?

   _____

   _____

2. Do I want my child to keep it? Is it in my child's greatest interest?

   _____

   _____

3. Did watching that trait make me laugh and smile?

   _____

   _____

4. Did the behavior trigger me? What would I like my child to exhibit instead?

   _____

   _____

To know thyself is the beginning of wisdom.
Socrates

5. Do I even see the behavior in myself? Am I willing to change or alter the same behavior in me?

_____

_____

6. What change do I need to make in myself to be a better role model, so my young one will exhibit **that** behavior instead?

_____

_____

_____

7. Time to take a moment to reflect on what I've learned about myself from my child. Jot down a few thoughts (i.e., wishes, hopes, courageousness, forgiveness, acceptance, encouragement, etc…) about me. What plan will I make to improve myself and become my child's best example?

_____

_____

_____

_____

TODAY'S DATE _____

CHILD'S NAME/AGE _____

_____

1. What behavior did my child exhibit today that caught my attention?

_____

_____

2. Do I want my child to keep it? Is it in my child's greatest interest?

_____

_____

3. Did watching that trait make me laugh and smile?

_____

_____

4. Did the behavior trigger me? What would I like my child to exhibit instead?

_____

_____

To know thyself is the beginning of wisdom.
Socrates

5. Do I even see the behavior in myself? Am I willing to change or alter the same behavior in me?

_____

_____

6. What change do I need to make in myself to be a better role model, so my young one will exhibit **that** behavior instead?

_____

_____

_____

7. Time to take a moment to reflect on what I've learned about myself from my child. Jot down a few thoughts (i.e., wishes, hopes, courageousness, forgiveness, acceptance, encouragement, etc...) about me. What plan will I make to improve myself and become my child's best example?

_____

_____

_____

_____

TODAY'S DATE _____

CHILD'S NAME/AGE _____

_____

1. What behavior did my child exhibit today that caught my attention?

_____

_____

2. Do I want my child to keep it? Is it in my child's greatest interest?

_____

_____

3. Did watching that trait make me laugh and smile?

_____

_____

4. Did the behavior trigger me? What would I like my child to exhibit instead?

_____

_____

To know thyself is the beginning of wisdom.
Socrates

5. Do I even see the behavior in myself? Am I willing to change or alter the same behavior in me?

_____
_____

6. What change do I need to make in myself to be a better role model, so my young one will exhibit **that** behavior instead?

_____
_____
_____

7. Time to take a moment to reflect on what I've learned about myself from my child. Jot down a few thoughts (i.e., wishes, hopes, courageousness, forgiveness, acceptance, encouragement, etc...) about me. What plan will I make to improve myself and become my child's best example?

_____
_____
_____
_____

TODAY'S DATE _____

CHILD'S NAME/AGE _____

_____

1. What behavior did my child exhibit today that caught my attention?

   _____

   _____

2. Do I want my child to keep it? Is it in my child's greatest interest?

   _____

   _____

3. Did watching that trait make me laugh and smile?

   _____

   _____

4. Did the behavior trigger me? What would I like my child to exhibit instead?

   _____

   _____

To know thyself is the beginning of wisdom.
Socrates

5. Do I even see the behavior in myself? Am I willing to change or alter the same behavior in me?

6. What change do I need to make in myself to be a better role model, so my young one will exhibit **that** behavior instead?

7. Time to take a moment to reflect on what I've learned about myself from my child. Jot down a few thoughts (i.e., wishes, hopes, courageousness, forgiveness, acceptance, encouragement, etc…) about me. What plan will I make to improve myself and become my child's best example?

TODAY'S DATE _____

CHILD'S NAME/AGE _____

_____

1. What behavior did my child exhibit today that caught my attention?

   _____

   _____

2. Do I want my child to keep it? Is it in my child's greatest interest?

   _____

   _____

3. Did watching that trait make me laugh and smile?

   _____

   _____

4. Did the behavior trigger me? What would I like my child to exhibit instead?

   _____

   _____

TO KNOW THYSELF IS THE BEGINNING OF WISDOM.

SOCRATES

5. Do I even see the behavior in myself? Am I willing to change or alter the same behavior in me?

_____
_____

6. What change do I need to make in myself to be a better role model, so my young one will exhibit **that** behavior instead?

_____
_____
_____

7. Time to take a moment to reflect on what I've learned about myself from my child. Jot down a few thoughts (i.e., wishes, hopes, courageousness, forgiveness, acceptance, encouragement, etc…) about me. What plan will I make to improve myself and become my child's best example?

_____
_____
_____
_____

TODAY'S DATE _____

CHILD'S NAME/AGE _____

_____

1. What behavior did my child exhibit today that caught my attention?

   _____
   _____

2. Do I want my child to keep it? Is it in my child's greatest interest?

   _____
   _____

3. Did watching that trait make me laugh and smile?

   _____
   _____

4. Did the behavior trigger me? What would I like my child to exhibit instead?

   _____
   _____

To know thyself is the beginning of wisdom.
Socrates

5. Do I even see the behavior in myself? Am I willing to change or alter the same behavior in me?

6. What change do I need to make in myself to be a better role model, so my young one will exhibit **that** behavior instead?

7. Time to take a moment to reflect on what I've learned about myself from my child. Jot down a few thoughts (i.e., wishes, hopes, courageousness, forgiveness, acceptance, encouragement, etc...) about me. What plan will I make to improve myself and become my child's best example?

TODAY'S DATE _____

CHILD'S NAME/AGE _____

_____

1. What behavior did my child exhibit today that caught my attention?

   _____

   _____

2. Do I want my child to keep it? Is it in my child's greatest interest?

   _____

   _____

3. Did watching that trait make me laugh and smile?

   _____

   _____

4. Did the behavior trigger me? What would I like my child to exhibit instead?

   _____

   _____

To know thyself is the beginning of wisdom.
Socrates

5. Do I even see the behavior in myself? Am I willing to change or alter the same behavior in me?

6. What change do I need to make in myself to be a better role model, so my young one will exhibit **that** behavior instead?

7. Time to take a moment to reflect on what I've learned about myself from my child. Jot down a few thoughts (i.e., wishes, hopes, courageousness, forgiveness, acceptance, encouragement, etc…) about me. What plan will I make to improve myself and become my child's best example?

TODAY'S DATE _____

CHILD'S NAME/AGE _____

_____

1. What behavior did my child exhibit today that caught my attention?

   _____

   _____

2. Do I want my child to keep it? Is it in my child's greatest interest?

   _____

   _____

3. Did watching that trait make me laugh and smile?

   _____

   _____

4. Did the behavior trigger me? What would I like my child to exhibit instead?

   _____

   _____

> To know thyself is the beginning of wisdom.
> Socrates

5. Do I even see the behavior in myself? Am I willing to change or alter the same behavior in me?

6. What change do I need to make in myself to be a better role model, so my young one will exhibit **that** behavior instead?

7. Time to take a moment to reflect on what I've learned about myself from my child. Jot down a few thoughts (i.e., wishes, hopes, courageousness, forgiveness, acceptance, encouragement, etc…) about me. What plan will I make to improve myself and become my child's best example?

TODAY'S DATE _____

CHILD'S NAME/AGE _____

_____

1. What behavior did my child exhibit today that caught my attention?

   _____
   _____

2. Do I want my child to keep it? Is it in my child's greatest interest?

   _____
   _____

3. Did watching that trait make me laugh and smile?

   _____
   _____

4. Did the behavior trigger me? What would I like my child to exhibit instead?

   _____
   _____

To know thyself is the beginning of wisdom.
Socrates

5. Do I even see the behavior in myself? Am I willing to change or alter the same behavior in me?

---

6. What change do I need to make in myself to be a better role model, so my young one will exhibit **that** behavior instead?

---

7. Time to take a moment to reflect on what I've learned about myself from my child. Jot down a few thoughts (i.e., wishes, hopes, courageousness, forgiveness, acceptance, encouragement, etc...) about me. What plan will I make to improve myself and become my child's best example?

TODAY'S DATE _____

CHILD'S NAME/AGE _____

_____

1. What behavior did my child exhibit today that caught my attention?

_____

_____

2. Do I want my child to keep it? Is it in my child's greatest interest?

_____

_____

3. Did watching that trait make me laugh and smile?

_____

_____

4. Did the behavior trigger me? What would I like my child to exhibit instead?

_____

_____

To know thyself is the beginning of wisdom.

Socrates

5. Do I even see the behavior in myself? Am I willing to change or alter the same behavior in me?

6. What change do I need to make in myself to be a better role model, so my young one will exhibit **that** behavior instead?

7. Time to take a moment to reflect on what I've learned about myself from my child. Jot down a few thoughts (i.e., wishes, hopes, courageousness, forgiveness, acceptance, encouragement, etc...) about me. What plan will I make to improve myself and become my child's best example?

TODAY'S DATE _____

CHILD'S NAME/AGE _____

_____

1. What behavior did my child exhibit today that caught my attention?

   _____
   _____

2. Do I want my child to keep it? Is it in my child's greatest interest?

   _____
   _____

3. Did watching that trait make me laugh and smile?

   _____
   _____

4. Did the behavior trigger me? What would I like my child to exhibit instead?

   _____
   _____

To know thyself is the beginning of wisdom.
Socrates

5. Do I even see the behavior in myself? Am I willing to change or alter the same behavior in me?

   _____
   _____

6. What change do I need to make in myself to be a better role model, so my young one will exhibit **that** behavior instead?

   _____
   _____
   _____

7. Time to take a moment to reflect on what I've learned about myself from my child. Jot down a few thoughts (i.e., wishes, hopes, courageousness, forgiveness, acceptance, encouragement, etc...) about me. What plan will I make to improve myself and become my child's best example?

   _____
   _____
   _____
   _____

TODAY'S DATE _____

CHILD'S NAME/AGE _____

_____

1. What behavior did my child exhibit today that caught my attention?

_____

_____

2. Do I want my child to keep it? Is it in my child's greatest interest?

_____

_____

3. Did watching that trait make me laugh and smile?

_____

_____

4. Did the behavior trigger me? What would I like my child to exhibit instead?

_____

_____

To know thyself is the beginning of wisdom.

Socrates

5. Do I even see the behavior in myself? Am I willing to change or alter the same behavior in me?

_____

_____

6. What change do I need to make in myself to be a better role model, so my young one will exhibit **that** behavior instead?

_____

_____

_____

7. Time to take a moment to reflect on what I've learned about myself from my child. Jot down a few thoughts (i.e., wishes, hopes, courageousness, forgiveness, acceptance, encouragement, etc...) about me. What plan will I make to improve myself and become my child's best example?

_____

_____

_____

_____

TODAY'S DATE _____

CHILD'S NAME/AGE _____

_____

1. What behavior did my child exhibit today that caught my attention?

___

___

2. Do I want my child to keep it? Is it in my child's greatest interest?

___

___

3. Did watching that trait make me laugh and smile?

___

___

4. Did the behavior trigger me? What would I like my child to exhibit instead?

___

___

To know thyself is the beginning of wisdom.
Socrates

5. Do I even see the behavior in myself? Am I willing to change or alter the same behavior in me?

6. What change do I need to make in myself to be a better role model, so my young one will exhibit **that** behavior instead?

7. Time to take a moment to reflect on what I've learned about myself from my child. Jot down a few thoughts (i.e., wishes, hopes, courageousness, forgiveness, acceptance, encouragement, etc...) about me. What plan will I make to improve myself and become my child's best example?

TODAY'S DATE _____

CHILD'S NAME/AGE _____

_____

1. What behavior did my child exhibit today that caught my attention?

   _____
   _____

2. Do I want my child to keep it? Is it in my child's greatest interest?

   _____
   _____

3. Did watching that trait make me laugh and smile?

   _____
   _____

4. Did the behavior trigger me? What would I like my child to exhibit instead?

   _____
   _____

To know thyself is the beginning of wisdom.
Socrates

5. Do I even see the behavior in myself? Am I willing to change or alter the same behavior in me?

6. What change do I need to make in myself to be a better role model, so my young one will exhibit **that** behavior instead?

7. Time to take a moment to reflect on what I've learned about myself from my child. Jot down a few thoughts (i.e., wishes, hopes, courageousness, forgiveness, acceptance, encouragement, etc…) about me. What plan will I make to improve myself and become my child's best example?

TODAY'S DATE _____

CHILD'S NAME/AGE _____

_____

1. What behavior did my child exhibit today that caught my attention?

_____

_____

2. Do I want my child to keep it? Is it in my child's greatest interest?

_____

_____

3. Did watching that trait make me laugh and smile?

_____

_____

4. Did the behavior trigger me? What would I like my child to exhibit instead?

_____

_____

TO KNOW THYSELF IS THE BEGINNING OF WISDOM.
SOCRATES

5. Do I even see the behavior in myself? Am I willing to change or alter the same behavior in me?

6. What change do I need to make in myself to be a better role model, so my young one will exhibit **that** behavior instead?

7. Time to take a moment to reflect on what I've learned about myself from my child. Jot down a few thoughts (i.e., wishes, hopes, courageousness, forgiveness, acceptance, encouragement, etc…) about me. What plan will I make to improve myself and become my child's best example?

TODAY'S DATE _____

CHILD'S NAME/AGE _____

_____

1. What behavior did my child exhibit today that caught my attention?

   _____

   _____

2. Do I want my child to keep it? Is it in my child's greatest interest?

   _____

   _____

3. Did watching that trait make me laugh and smile?

   _____

   _____

4. Did the behavior trigger me? What would I like my child to exhibit instead?

   _____

   _____

To know thyself is the beginning of wisdom.
Socrates

5. Do I even see the behavior in myself? Am I willing to change or alter the same behavior in me?

_____

_____

6. What change do I need to make in myself to be a better role model, so my young one will exhibit **that** behavior instead?

_____

_____

_____

7. Time to take a moment to reflect on what I've learned about myself from my child. Jot down a few thoughts (i.e., wishes, hopes, courageousness, forgiveness, acceptance, encouragement, etc...) about me. What plan will I make to improve myself and become my child's best example?

_____

_____

_____

_____

TODAY'S DATE _____

CHILD'S NAME/AGE _____

_____

1. What behavior did my child exhibit today that caught my attention?

   _____

   _____

2. Do I want my child to keep it? Is it in my child's greatest interest?

   _____

   _____

3. Did watching that trait make me laugh and smile?

   _____

   _____

4. Did the behavior trigger me? What would I like my child to exhibit instead?

   _____

   _____

To know thyself is the beginning of wisdom.
Socrates

5. Do I even see the behavior in myself? Am I willing to change or alter the same behavior in me?

_____

_____

6. What change do I need to make in myself to be a better role model, so my young one will exhibit **that** behavior instead?

_____

_____

_____

7. Time to take a moment to reflect on what I've learned about myself from my child. Jot down a few thoughts (i.e., wishes, hopes, courageousness, forgiveness, acceptance, encouragement, etc…) about me. What plan will I make to improve myself and become my child's best example?

_____

_____

_____

_____

TODAY'S DATE _____

CHILD'S NAME/AGE _____

_____

1. What behavior did my child exhibit today that caught my attention?

   _____

   _____

2. Do I want my child to keep it? Is it in my child's greatest interest?

   _____

   _____

3. Did watching that trait make me laugh and smile?

   _____

   _____

4. Did the behavior trigger me? What would I like my child to exhibit instead?

   _____

   _____

To know thyself is the beginning of wisdom.
Socrates

DAILY PARENTING REFLECTIONS

5. Do I even see the behavior in myself? Am I willing to change or alter the same behavior in me?

_____

_____

6. What change do I need to make in myself to be a better role model, so my young one will exhibit **that** behavior instead?

_____

_____

_____

7. Time to take a moment to reflect on what I've learned about myself from my child. Jot down a few thoughts (i.e., wishes, hopes, courageousness, forgiveness, acceptance, encouragement, etc...) about me. What plan will I make to improve myself and become my child's best example?

_____

_____

_____

_____

TODAY'S DATE _____

CHILD'S NAME/AGE _____

_____

1. What behavior did my child exhibit today that caught my attention?

   _____

   _____

2. Do I want my child to keep it? Is it in my child's greatest interest?

   _____

   _____

3. Did watching that trait make me laugh and smile?

   _____

   _____

4. Did the behavior trigger me? What would I like my child to exhibit instead?

   _____

   _____

To know thyself is the beginning of wisdom.
Socrates

5. Do I even see the behavior in myself? Am I willing to change or alter the same behavior in me?

_____

_____

6. What change do I need to make in myself to be a better role model, so my young one will exhibit **that** behavior instead?

_____

_____

_____

7. Time to take a moment to reflect on what I've learned about myself from my child. Jot down a few thoughts (i.e., wishes, hopes, courageousness, forgiveness, acceptance, encouragement, etc…) about me. What plan will I make to improve myself and become my child's best example?

_____

_____

_____

_____

TODAY'S DATE _____

CHILD'S NAME/AGE _____

_____

1. What behavior did my child exhibit today that caught my attention?

   _____
   _____

2. Do I want my child to keep it? Is it in my child's greatest interest?

   _____
   _____

3. Did watching that trait make me laugh and smile?

   _____
   _____

4. Did the behavior trigger me? What would I like my child to exhibit instead?

   _____
   _____

To know thyself is the beginning of wisdom.
Socrates

5. Do I even see the behavior in myself? Am I willing to change or alter the same behavior in me?

_____

_____

6. What change do I need to make in myself to be a better role model, so my young one will exhibit **that** behavior instead?

_____

_____

_____

7. Time to take a moment to reflect on what I've learned about myself from my child. Jot down a few thoughts (i.e., wishes, hopes, courageousness, forgiveness, acceptance, encouragement, etc…) about me. What plan will I make to improve myself and become my child's best example?

_____

_____

_____

_____

TODAY'S DATE _____

CHILD'S NAME/AGE _____

_____

1. What behavior did my child exhibit today that caught my attention?

   _____
   _____

2. Do I want my child to keep it? Is it in my child's greatest interest?

   _____
   _____

3. Did watching that trait make me laugh and smile?

   _____
   _____

4. Did the behavior trigger me? What would I like my child to exhibit instead?

   _____
   _____

To know thyself is the beginning of wisdom.
Socrates

5. Do I even see the behavior in myself? Am I willing to change or alter the same behavior in me?

___

___

6. What change do I need to make in myself to be a better role model, so my young one will exhibit **that** behavior instead?

___

___

___

7. Time to take a moment to reflect on what I've learned about myself from my child. Jot down a few thoughts (i.e., wishes, hopes, courageousness, forgiveness, acceptance, encouragement, etc...) about me. What plan will I make to improve myself and become my child's best example?

___

___

___

___

TODAY'S DATE _____

CHILD'S NAME/AGE _____

_____

1. What behavior did my child exhibit today that caught my attention?

   _____

   _____

2. Do I want my child to keep it? Is it in my child's greatest interest?

   _____

   _____

3. Did watching that trait make me laugh and smile?

   _____

   _____

4. Did the behavior trigger me? What would I like my child to exhibit instead?

   _____

   _____

To know thyself is the beginning of wisdom.
Socrates

5. Do I even see the behavior in myself? Am I willing to change or alter the same behavior in me?

_____

_____

6. What change do I need to make in myself to be a better role model, so my young one will exhibit **that** behavior instead?

_____

_____

_____

7. Time to take a moment to reflect on what I've learned about myself from my child. Jot down a few thoughts (i.e., wishes, hopes, courageousness, forgiveness, acceptance, encouragement, etc…) about me. What plan will I make to improve myself and become my child's best example?

_____

_____

_____

_____

TODAY'S DATE _____
CHILD'S NAME/AGE _____
_____

1. What behavior did my child exhibit today that caught my attention?

   _____

   _____

2. Do I want my child to keep it? Is it in my child's greatest interest?

   _____

   _____

3. Did watching that trait make me laugh and smile?

   _____

   _____

4. Did the behavior trigger me? What would I like my child to exhibit instead?

   _____

   _____

To know thyself is the beginning of wisdom.

Socrates

5. Do I even see the behavior in myself? Am I willing to change or alter the same behavior in me?

_____

_____

6. What change do I need to make in myself to be a better role model, so my young one will exhibit **that** behavior instead?

_____

_____

_____

7. Time to take a moment to reflect on what I've learned about myself from my child. Jot down a few thoughts (i.e., wishes, hopes, courageousness, forgiveness, acceptance, encouragement, etc...) about me. What plan will I make to improve myself and become my child's best example?

_____

_____

_____

_____

TODAY'S DATE _____

CHILD'S NAME/AGE _____

_____

1. What behavior did my child exhibit today that caught my attention?

   _____

   _____

2. Do I want my child to keep it? Is it in my child's greatest interest?

   _____

   _____

3. Did watching that trait make me laugh and smile?

   _____

   _____

4. Did the behavior trigger me? What would I like my child to exhibit instead?

   _____

   _____

> TO KNOW THYSELF IS THE BEGINNING OF WISDOM.
> SOCRATES

5. Do I even see the behavior in myself? Am I willing to change or alter the same behavior in me?

___

___

6. What change do I need to make in myself to be a better role model, so my young one will exhibit **that** behavior instead?

___

___

___

7. Time to take a moment to reflect on what I've learned about myself from my child. Jot down a few thoughts (i.e., wishes, hopes, courageousness, forgiveness, acceptance, encouragement, etc...) about me. What plan will I make to improve myself and become my child's best example?

___

___

___

___

TODAY'S DATE _____

CHILD'S NAME/AGE _____

_____

1. What behavior did my child exhibit today that caught my attention?

_____

_____

2. Do I want my child to keep it? Is it in my child's greatest interest?

_____

_____

3. Did watching that trait make me laugh and smile?

_____

_____

4. Did the behavior trigger me? What would I like my child to exhibit instead?

_____

_____

TO KNOW THYSELF IS THE BEGINNING OF WISDOM.
SOCRATES

5. Do I even see the behavior in myself? Am I willing to change or alter the same behavior in me?

6. What change do I need to make in myself to be a better role model, so my young one will exhibit **that** behavior instead?

7. Time to take a moment to reflect on what I've learned about myself from my child. Jot down a few thoughts (i.e., wishes, hopes, courageousness, forgiveness, acceptance, encouragement, etc...) about me. What plan will I make to improve myself and become my child's best example?

TODAY'S DATE _____

CHILD'S NAME/AGE _____

_____

1. What behavior did my child exhibit today that caught my attention?

   _____
   _____

2. Do I want my child to keep it? Is it in my child's greatest interest?

   _____
   _____

3. Did watching that trait make me laugh and smile?

   _____
   _____

4. Did the behavior trigger me? What would I like my child to exhibit instead?

   _____
   _____

To know thyself is the beginning of wisdom.
Socrates

5. Do I even see the behavior in myself? Am I willing to change or alter the same behavior in me?

_____
_____

6. What change do I need to make in myself to be a better role model, so my young one will exhibit **that** behavior instead?

_____
_____
_____

7. Time to take a moment to reflect on what I've learned about myself from my child. Jot down a few thoughts (i.e., wishes, hopes, courageousness, forgiveness, acceptance, encouragement, etc...) about me. What plan will I make to improve myself and become my child's best example?

_____
_____
_____
_____

TODAY'S DATE _____

CHILD'S NAME/AGE _____

_____

1. What behavior did my child exhibit today that caught my attention?

   _____

   _____

2. Do I want my child to keep it? Is it in my child's greatest interest?

   _____

   _____

3. Did watching that trait make me laugh and smile?

   _____

   _____

4. Did the behavior trigger me? What would I like my child to exhibit instead?

   _____

   _____

TO KNOW THYSELF IS THE BEGINNING OF WISDOM.

SOCRATES

5. Do I even see the behavior in myself? Am I willing to change or alter the same behavior in me?

_____

_____

6. What change do I need to make in myself to be a better role model, so my young one will exhibit **that** behavior instead?

_____

_____

_____

7. Time to take a moment to reflect on what I've learned about myself from my child. Jot down a few thoughts (i.e., wishes, hopes, courageousness, forgiveness, acceptance, encouragement, etc...) about me. What plan will I make to improve myself and become my child's best example?

_____

_____

_____

_____

TODAY'S DATE _____

CHILD'S NAME/AGE _____

_____

1. What behavior did my child exhibit today that caught my attention?

   _____
   _____

2. Do I want my child to keep it? Is it in my child's greatest interest?

   _____
   _____

3. Did watching that trait make me laugh and smile?

   _____
   _____

4. Did the behavior trigger me? What would I like my child to exhibit instead?

   _____
   _____

To know thyself is the beginning of wisdom.
Socrates

5. Do I even see the behavior in myself? Am I willing to change or alter the same behavior in me?

6. What change do I need to make in myself to be a better role model, so my young one will exhibit **that** behavior instead?

7. Time to take a moment to reflect on what I've learned about myself from my child. Jot down a few thoughts (i.e., wishes, hopes, courageousness, forgiveness, acceptance, encouragement, etc...) about me. What plan will I make to improve myself and become my child's best example?

TODAY'S DATE _____

CHILD'S NAME/AGE _____

_____

1. What behavior did my child exhibit today that caught my attention?

   _____

   _____

2. Do I want my child to keep it? Is it in my child's greatest interest?

   _____

   _____

3. Did watching that trait make me laugh and smile?

   _____

   _____

4. Did the behavior trigger me? What would I like my child to exhibit instead?

   _____

   _____

To know thyself is the beginning of wisdom.

Socrates

5. Do I even see the behavior in myself? Am I willing to change or alter the same behavior in me?

_____

_____

6. What change do I need to make in myself to be a better role model, so my young one will exhibit **that** behavior instead?

_____

_____

_____

7. Time to take a moment to reflect on what I've learned about myself from my child. Jot down a few thoughts (i.e., wishes, hopes, courageousness, forgiveness, acceptance, encouragement, etc…) about me. What plan will I make to improve myself and become my child's best example?

_____

_____

_____

_____

TODAY'S DATE _____

CHILD'S NAME/AGE _____

_____

1. What behavior did my child exhibit today that caught my attention?

   _____

   _____

2. Do I want my child to keep it? Is it in my child's greatest interest?

   _____

   _____

3. Did watching that trait make me laugh and smile?

   _____

   _____

4. Did the behavior trigger me? What would I like my child to exhibit instead?

   _____

   _____

To know thyself is the beginning of wisdom.
Socrates

5. Do I even see the behavior in myself? Am I willing to change or alter the same behavior in me?

6. What change do I need to make in myself to be a better role model, so my young one will exhibit **that** behavior instead?

7. Time to take a moment to reflect on what I've learned about myself from my child. Jot down a few thoughts (i.e., wishes, hopes, courageousness, forgiveness, acceptance, encouragement, etc...) about me. What plan will I make to improve myself and become my child's best example?

TODAY'S DATE _____

CHILD'S NAME/AGE _____

_____

1. What behavior did my child exhibit today that caught my attention?

   _____

   _____

2. Do I want my child to keep it? Is it in my child's greatest interest?

   _____

   _____

3. Did watching that trait make me laugh and smile?

   _____

   _____

4. Did the behavior trigger me? What would I like my child to exhibit instead?

   _____

   _____

To know thyself is the beginning of wisdom.
Socrates

5. Do I even see the behavior in myself? Am I willing to change or alter the same behavior in me?

_____

_____

6. What change do I need to make in myself to be a better role model, so my young one will exhibit **that** behavior instead?

_____

_____

_____

7. Time to take a moment to reflect on what I've learned about myself from my child. Jot down a few thoughts (i.e., wishes, hopes, courageousness, forgiveness, acceptance, encouragement, etc...) about me. What plan will I make to improve myself and become my child's best example?

_____

_____

_____

_____

TODAY'S DATE _____

CHILD'S NAME/AGE _____

_____

1. What behavior did my child exhibit today that caught my attention?

   _____

   _____

2. Do I want my child to keep it? Is it in my child's greatest interest?

   _____

   _____

3. Did watching that trait make me laugh and smile?

   _____

   _____

4. Did the behavior trigger me? What would I like my child to exhibit instead?

   _____

   _____

TO KNOW THYSELF IS THE BEGINNING OF WISDOM.
SOCRATES

5. Do I even see the behavior in myself? Am I willing to change or alter the same behavior in me?

_____

_____

6. What change do I need to make in myself to be a better role model, so my young one will exhibit **that** behavior instead?

_____

_____

_____

7. Time to take a moment to reflect on what I've learned about myself from my child. Jot down a few thoughts (i.e., wishes, hopes, courageousness, forgiveness, acceptance, encouragement, etc...) about me. What plan will I make to improve myself and become my child's best example?

_____

_____

_____

_____

TODAY'S DATE _____

CHILD'S NAME/AGE _____

_____

1. What behavior did my child exhibit today that caught my attention?

   _____

   _____

2. Do I want my child to keep it? Is it in my child's greatest interest?

   _____

   _____

3. Did watching that trait make me laugh and smile?

   _____

   _____

4. Did the behavior trigger me? What would I like my child to exhibit instead?

   _____

   _____

To know thyself is the beginning of wisdom.

Socrates

5. Do I even see the behavior in myself? Am I willing to change or alter the same behavior in me?

_____

_____

6. What change do I need to make in myself to be a better role model, so my young one will exhibit **that** behavior instead?

_____

_____

_____

7. Time to take a moment to reflect on what I've learned about myself from my child. Jot down a few thoughts (i.e., wishes, hopes, courageousness, forgiveness, acceptance, encouragement, etc...) about me. What plan will I make to improve myself and become my child's best example?

_____

_____

_____

_____

TODAY'S DATE _____

CHILD'S NAME/AGE _____

_____

1. What behavior did my child exhibit today that caught my attention?

   _____

   _____

2. Do I want my child to keep it? Is it in my child's greatest interest?

   _____

   _____

3. Did watching that trait make me laugh and smile?

   _____

   _____

4. Did the behavior trigger me? What would I like my child to exhibit instead?

   _____

   _____

TO KNOW THYSELF IS THE BEGINNING OF WISDOM.
SOCRATES

5. Do I even see the behavior in myself? Am I willing to change or alter the same behavior in me?

6. What change do I need to make in myself to be a better role model, so my young one will exhibit **that** behavior instead?

7. Time to take a moment to reflect on what I've learned about myself from my child. Jot down a few thoughts (i.e., wishes, hopes, courageousness, forgiveness, acceptance, encouragement, etc…) about me. What plan will I make to improve myself and become my child's best example?

TODAY'S DATE _____

CHILD'S NAME/AGE _____

_____

1. What behavior did my child exhibit today that caught my attention?

   _____

   _____

2. Do I want my child to keep it? Is it in my child's greatest interest?

   _____

   _____

3. Did watching that trait make me laugh and smile?

   _____

   _____

4. Did the behavior trigger me? What would I like my child to exhibit instead?

   _____

   _____

To know thyself is the beginning of wisdom.
Socrates

5. Do I even see the behavior in myself? Am I willing to change or alter the same behavior in me?

_____

_____

6. What change do I need to make in myself to be a better role model, so my young one will exhibit **that** behavior instead?

_____

_____

7. Time to take a moment to reflect on what I've learned about myself from my child. Jot down a few thoughts (i.e., wishes, hopes, courageousness, forgiveness, acceptance, encouragement, etc…) about me. What plan will I make to improve myself and become my child's best example?

_____

_____

_____

_____

TODAY'S DATE _____

CHILD'S NAME/AGE _____

_____

1. What behavior did my child exhibit today that caught my attention?

   _____

   _____

2. Do I want my child to keep it? Is it in my child's greatest interest?

   _____

   _____

3. Did watching that trait make me laugh and smile?

   _____

   _____

4. Did the behavior trigger me? What would I like my child to exhibit instead?

   _____

   _____

> To know thyself is the beginning of wisdom.
> Socrates

5. Do I even see the behavior in myself? Am I willing to change or alter the same behavior in me?

6. What change do I need to make in myself to be a better role model, so my young one will exhibit **that** behavior instead?

7. Time to take a moment to reflect on what I've learned about myself from my child. Jot down a few thoughts (i.e., wishes, hopes, courageousness, forgiveness, acceptance, encouragement, etc…) about me. What plan will I make to improve myself and become my child's best example?

TODAY'S DATE _____

CHILD'S NAME/AGE _____

_____

1. What behavior did my child exhibit today that caught my attention?

   _____

   _____

2. Do I want my child to keep it? Is it in my child's greatest interest?

   _____

   _____

3. Did watching that trait make me laugh and smile?

   _____

   _____

4. Did the behavior trigger me? What would I like my child to exhibit instead?

   _____

   _____

To know thyself is the beginning of wisdom.

Socrates

5. Do I even see the behavior in myself? Am I willing to change or alter the same behavior in me?

_____

_____

6. What change do I need to make in myself to be a better role model, so my young one will exhibit **that** behavior instead?

_____

_____

_____

7. Time to take a moment to reflect on what I've learned about myself from my child. Jot down a few thoughts (i.e., wishes, hopes, courageousness, forgiveness, acceptance, encouragement, etc...) about me. What plan will I make to improve myself and become my child's best example?

_____

_____

_____

_____

TODAY'S DATE _____

CHILD'S NAME/AGE _____

_____

1. What behavior did my child exhibit today that caught my attention?

   _____
   _____

2. Do I want my child to keep it? Is it in my child's greatest interest?

   _____
   _____

3. Did watching that trait make me laugh and smile?

   _____
   _____

4. Did the behavior trigger me? What would I like my child to exhibit instead?

   _____
   _____

To know thyself is the beginning of wisdom.
Socrates

5. Do I even see the behavior in myself? Am I willing to change or alter the same behavior in me?

6. What change do I need to make in myself to be a better role model, so my young one will exhibit **that** behavior instead?

7. Time to take a moment to reflect on what I've learned about myself from my child. Jot down a few thoughts (i.e., wishes, hopes, courageousness, forgiveness, acceptance, encouragement, etc…) about me. What plan will I make to improve myself and become my child's best example?

TODAY'S DATE _____

CHILD'S NAME/AGE _____

_____

1. What behavior did my child exhibit today that caught my attention?

   _____

   _____

2. Do I want my child to keep it? Is it in my child's greatest interest?

   _____

   _____

3. Did watching that trait make me laugh and smile?

   _____

   _____

4. Did the behavior trigger me? What would I like my child to exhibit instead?

   _____

   _____

TO KNOW THYSELF IS THE BEGINNING OF WISDOM.

SOCRATES

5. Do I even see the behavior in myself? Am I willing to change or alter the same behavior in me?

6. What change do I need to make in myself to be a better role model, so my young one will exhibit **that** behavior instead?

7. Time to take a moment to reflect on what I've learned about myself from my child. Jot down a few thoughts (i.e., wishes, hopes, courageousness, forgiveness, acceptance, encouragement, etc...) about me. What plan will I make to improve myself and become my child's best example?

TODAY'S DATE _____

CHILD'S NAME/AGE _____

_____

1. What behavior did my child exhibit today that caught my attention?

_____
_____

2. Do I want my child to keep it? Is it in my child's greatest interest?

_____
_____

3. Did watching that trait make me laugh and smile?

_____
_____

4. Did the behavior trigger me? What would I like my child to exhibit instead?

_____
_____

To know thyself is the beginning of wisdom.
Socrates

5. Do I even see the behavior in myself? Am I willing to change or alter the same behavior in me?

___

6. What change do I need to make in myself to be a better role model, so my young one will exhibit **that** behavior instead?

___

7. Time to take a moment to reflect on what I've learned about myself from my child. Jot down a few thoughts (i.e., wishes, hopes, courageousness, forgiveness, acceptance, encouragement, etc...) about me. What plan will I make to improve myself and become my child's best example?

___

TODAY'S DATE _____

CHILD'S NAME/AGE _____

_____

1. What behavior did my child exhibit today that caught my attention?

_____

_____

2. Do I want my child to keep it? Is it in my child's greatest interest?

_____

_____

3. Did watching that trait make me laugh and smile?

_____

_____

4. Did the behavior trigger me? What would I like my child to exhibit instead?

_____

_____

TO KNOW THYSELF IS THE BEGINNING OF WISDOM.

SOCRATES

5. Do I even see the behavior in myself? Am I willing to change or alter the same behavior in me?

6. What change do I need to make in myself to be a better role model, so my young one will exhibit **that** behavior instead?

7. Time to take a moment to reflect on what I've learned about myself from my child. Jot down a few thoughts (i.e., wishes, hopes, courageousness, forgiveness, acceptance, encouragement, etc…) about me. What plan will I make to improve myself and become my child's best example?

TODAY'S DATE   _____
CHILD'S NAME/AGE   _____
_____

1. What behavior did my child exhibit today that caught my attention?

    _____
    _____

2. Do I want my child to keep it? Is it in my child's greatest interest?

    _____
    _____

3. Did watching that trait make me laugh and smile?

    _____
    _____

4. Did the behavior trigger me? What would I like my child to exhibit instead?

    _____
    _____

To know thyself is the beginning of wisdom.
Socrates

5. Do I even see the behavior in myself? Am I willing to change or alter the same behavior in me?

6. What change do I need to make in myself to be a better role model, so my young one will exhibit **that** behavior instead?

7. Time to take a moment to reflect on what I've learned about myself from my child. Jot down a few thoughts (i.e., wishes, hopes, courageousness, forgiveness, acceptance, encouragement, etc...) about me. What plan will I make to improve myself and become my child's best example?

TODAY'S DATE _____

CHILD'S NAME/AGE _____

_____

1. What behavior did my child exhibit today that caught my attention?

   _____
   _____

2. Do I want my child to keep it? Is it in my child's greatest interest?

   _____
   _____

3. Did watching that trait make me laugh and smile?

   _____
   _____

4. Did the behavior trigger me? What would I like my child to exhibit instead?

   _____
   _____

To know thyself is the beginning of wisdom.
Socrates

5. Do I even see the behavior in myself? Am I willing to change or alter the same behavior in me?

_____

_____

6. What change do I need to make in myself to be a better role model, so my young one will exhibit **that** behavior instead?

_____

_____

_____

7. Time to take a moment to reflect on what I've learned about myself from my child. Jot down a few thoughts (i.e., wishes, hopes, courageousness, forgiveness, acceptance, encouragement, etc...) about me. What plan will I make to improve myself and become my child's best example?

_____

_____

_____

_____

TODAY'S DATE _____

CHILD'S NAME/AGE _____

_____

1. What behavior did my child exhibit today that caught my attention?

   _____
   _____

2. Do I want my child to keep it? Is it in my child's greatest interest?

   _____
   _____

3. Did watching that trait make me laugh and smile?

   _____
   _____

4. Did the behavior trigger me? What would I like my child to exhibit instead?

   _____
   _____

To know thyself is the beginning of wisdom.
Socrates

5. Do I even see the behavior in myself? Am I willing to change or alter the same behavior in me?

6. What change do I need to make in myself to be a better role model, so my young one will exhibit **that** behavior instead?

7. Time to take a moment to reflect on what I've learned about myself from my child. Jot down a few thoughts (i.e., wishes, hopes, courageousness, forgiveness, acceptance, encouragement, etc...) about me. What plan will I make to improve myself and become my child's best example?

TODAY'S DATE _____

CHILD'S NAME/AGE _____

_____

1. What behavior did my child exhibit today that caught my attention?

   _____
   _____

2. Do I want my child to keep it? Is it in my child's greatest interest?

   _____
   _____

3. Did watching that trait make me laugh and smile?

   _____
   _____

4. Did the behavior trigger me? What would I like my child to exhibit instead?

   _____
   _____

TO KNOW THYSELF IS THE BEGINNING OF WISDOM.
SOCRATES

5. Do I even see the behavior in myself? Am I willing to change or alter the same behavior in me?

6. What change do I need to make in myself to be a better role model, so my young one will exhibit **that** behavior instead?

7. Time to take a moment to reflect on what I've learned about myself from my child. Jot down a few thoughts (i.e., wishes, hopes, courageousness, forgiveness, acceptance, encouragement, etc...) about me. What plan will I make to improve myself and become my child's best example?

TODAY'S DATE _____

CHILD'S NAME/AGE _____

_____

1. What behavior did my child exhibit today that caught my attention?

    _____

    _____

2. Do I want my child to keep it? Is it in my child's greatest interest?

    _____

    _____

3. Did watching that trait make me laugh and smile?

    _____

    _____

4. Did the behavior trigger me? What would I like my child to exhibit instead?

    _____

    _____

To know thyself is the beginning of wisdom.
Socrates

5. Do I even see the behavior in myself? Am I willing to change or alter the same behavior in me?

_____
_____

6. What change do I need to make in myself to be a better role model, so my young one will exhibit **that** behavior instead?

_____
_____
_____

7. Time to take a moment to reflect on what I've learned about myself from my child. Jot down a few thoughts (i.e., wishes, hopes, courageousness, forgiveness, acceptance, encouragement, etc...) about me. What plan will I make to improve myself and become my child's best example?

_____
_____
_____
_____

TODAY'S DATE _____

CHILD'S NAME/AGE _____

_____

1. What behavior did my child exhibit today that caught my attention?

   _____

   _____

2. Do I want my child to keep it? Is it in my child's greatest interest?

   _____

   _____

3. Did watching that trait make me laugh and smile?

   _____

   _____

4. Did the behavior trigger me? What would I like my child to exhibit instead?

   _____

   _____

TO KNOW THYSELF IS THE BEGINNING OF WISDOM.
SOCRATES

5. Do I even see the behavior in myself? Am I willing to change or alter the same behavior in me?

6. What change do I need to make in myself to be a better role model, so my young one will exhibit **that** behavior instead?

7. Time to take a moment to reflect on what I've learned about myself from my child. Jot down a few thoughts (i.e., wishes, hopes, courageousness, forgiveness, acceptance, encouragement, etc...) about me. What plan will I make to improve myself and become my child's best example?

TODAY'S DATE _____

CHILD'S NAME/AGE _____

_____

1. What behavior did my child exhibit today that caught my attention?

   _____

   _____

2. Do I want my child to keep it? Is it in my child's greatest interest?

   _____

   _____

3. Did watching that trait make me laugh and smile?

   _____

   _____

4. Did the behavior trigger me? What would I like my child to exhibit instead?

   _____

   _____

TO KNOW THYSELF IS THE BEGINNING OF WISDOM.
SOCRATES

5. Do I even see the behavior in myself? Am I willing to change or alter the same behavior in me?

_____

_____

6. What change do I need to make in myself to be a better role model, so my young one will exhibit **that** behavior instead?

_____

_____

_____

7. Time to take a moment to reflect on what I've learned about myself from my child. Jot down a few thoughts (i.e., wishes, hopes, courageousness, forgiveness, acceptance, encouragement, etc…) about me. What plan will I make to improve myself and become my child's best example?

_____

_____

_____

_____

TODAY'S DATE _____

CHILD'S NAME/AGE _____

_____

1. What behavior did my child exhibit today that caught my attention?

   _____

   _____

2. Do I want my child to keep it? Is it in my child's greatest interest?

   _____

   _____

3. Did watching that trait make me laugh and smile?

   _____

   _____

4. Did the behavior trigger me? What would I like my child to exhibit instead?

   _____

   _____

TO KNOW THYSELF IS THE BEGINNING OF WISDOM.

SOCRATES

5. Do I even see the behavior in myself? Am I willing to change or alter the same behavior in me?

_____
_____

6. What change do I need to make in myself to be a better role model, so my young one will exhibit **that** behavior instead?

_____
_____
_____

7. Time to take a moment to reflect on what I've learned about myself from my child. Jot down a few thoughts (i.e., wishes, hopes, courageousness, forgiveness, acceptance, encouragement, etc...) about me. What plan will I make to improve myself and become my child's best example?

_____
_____
_____
_____

TODAY'S DATE _____

CHILD'S NAME/AGE _____

_____

1. What behavior did my child exhibit today that caught my attention?

_____

_____

2. Do I want my child to keep it? Is it in my child's greatest interest?

_____

_____

3. Did watching that trait make me laugh and smile?

_____

_____

4. Did the behavior trigger me? What would I like my child to exhibit instead?

_____

_____

To know thyself is the beginning of wisdom.
Socrates

5. Do I even see the behavior in myself? Am I willing to change or alter the same behavior in me?

6. What change do I need to make in myself to be a better role model, so my young one will exhibit **that** behavior instead?

7. Time to take a moment to reflect on what I've learned about myself from my child. Jot down a few thoughts (i.e., wishes, hopes, courageousness, forgiveness, acceptance, encouragement, etc…) about me. What plan will I make to improve myself and become my child's best example?

TODAY'S DATE _____

CHILD'S NAME/AGE _____

_____

1. What behavior did my child exhibit today that caught my attention?

   _____

   _____

2. Do I want my child to keep it? Is it in my child's greatest interest?

   _____

   _____

3. Did watching that trait make me laugh and smile?

   _____

   _____

4. Did the behavior trigger me? What would I like my child to exhibit instead?

   _____

   _____

TO KNOW THYSELF IS THE BEGINNING OF WISDOM.

SOCRATES

5. Do I even see the behavior in myself? Am I willing to change or alter the same behavior in me?

   _____

   _____

6. What change do I need to make in myself to be a better role model, so my young one will exhibit **that** behavior instead?

   _____

   _____

   _____

7. Time to take a moment to reflect on what I've learned about myself from my child. Jot down a few thoughts (i.e., wishes, hopes, courageousness, forgiveness, acceptance, encouragement, etc…) about me. What plan will I make to improve myself and become my child's best example?

   _____

   _____

   _____

   _____

TODAY'S DATE _____

CHILD'S NAME/AGE _____

_____

1. What behavior did my child exhibit today that caught my attention?

_____

_____

2. Do I want my child to keep it? Is it in my child's greatest interest?

_____

_____

3. Did watching that trait make me laugh and smile?

_____

_____

4. Did the behavior trigger me? What would I like my child to exhibit instead?

_____

_____

To know thyself is the beginning of wisdom.
Socrates

5. Do I even see the behavior in myself? Am I willing to change or alter the same behavior in me?

_____

_____

6. What change do I need to make in myself to be a better role model, so my young one will exhibit **that** behavior instead?

_____

_____

_____

7. Time to take a moment to reflect on what I've learned about myself from my child. Jot down a few thoughts (i.e., wishes, hopes, courageousness, forgiveness, acceptance, encouragement, etc...) about me. What plan will I make to improve myself and become my child's best example?

_____

_____

_____

_____

TODAY'S DATE _____

CHILD'S NAME/AGE _____

_____

1. What behavior did my child exhibit today that caught my attention?

_____

_____

2. Do I want my child to keep it? Is it in my child's greatest interest?

_____

_____

3. Did watching that trait make me laugh and smile?

_____

_____

4. Did the behavior trigger me? What would I like my child to exhibit instead?

_____

_____

To know thyself is the beginning of wisdom.
Socrates

5. Do I even see the behavior in myself? Am I willing to change or alter the same behavior in me?

6. What change do I need to make in myself to be a better role model, so my young one will exhibit **that** behavior instead?

7. Time to take a moment to reflect on what I've learned about myself from my child. Jot down a few thoughts (i.e., wishes, hopes, courageousness, forgiveness, acceptance, encouragement, etc…) about me. What plan will I make to improve myself and become my child's best example?

TODAY'S DATE _____

CHILD'S NAME/AGE _____

_____

1. What behavior did my child exhibit today that caught my attention?

   _____

   _____

2. Do I want my child to keep it? Is it in my child's greatest interest?

   _____

   _____

3. Did watching that trait make me laugh and smile?

   _____

   _____

4. Did the behavior trigger me? What would I like my child to exhibit instead?

   _____

   _____

TO KNOW THYSELF IS THE BEGINNING OF WISDOM.
SOCRATES

5. Do I even see the behavior in myself? Am I willing to change or alter the same behavior in me?

6. What change do I need to make in myself to be a better role model, so my young one will exhibit **that** behavior instead?

7. Time to take a moment to reflect on what I've learned about myself from my child. Jot down a few thoughts (i.e., wishes, hopes, courageousness, forgiveness, acceptance, encouragement, etc…) about me. What plan will I make to improve myself and become my child's best example?

TODAY'S DATE _____

CHILD'S NAME/AGE _____

_____

1. What behavior did my child exhibit today that caught my attention?

   _____
   _____

2. Do I want my child to keep it? Is it in my child's greatest interest?

   _____
   _____

3. Did watching that trait make me laugh and smile?

   _____
   _____

4. Did the behavior trigger me? What would I like my child to exhibit instead?

   _____
   _____

TO KNOW THYSELF IS THE BEGINNING OF WISDOM.
SOCRATES

5. Do I even see the behavior in myself? Am I willing to change or alter the same behavior in me?

6. What change do I need to make in myself to be a better role model, so my young one will exhibit **that** behavior instead?

7. Time to take a moment to reflect on what I've learned about myself from my child. Jot down a few thoughts (i.e., wishes, hopes, courageousness, forgiveness, acceptance, encouragement, etc…) about me. What plan will I make to improve myself and become my child's best example?

TODAY'S DATE _____

CHILD'S NAME/AGE _____

_____

1. What behavior did my child exhibit today that caught my attention?

   _____
   _____

2. Do I want my child to keep it? Is it in my child's greatest interest?

   _____
   _____

3. Did watching that trait make me laugh and smile?

   _____
   _____

4. Did the behavior trigger me? What would I like my child to exhibit instead?

   _____
   _____

TO KNOW THYSELF IS THE BEGINNING OF WISDOM.
SOCRATES

5. Do I even see the behavior in myself? Am I willing to change or alter the same behavior in me?

_____

_____

6. What change do I need to make in myself to be a better role model, so my young one will exhibit **that** behavior instead?

_____

_____

_____

7. Time to take a moment to reflect on what I've learned about myself from my child. Jot down a few thoughts (i.e., wishes, hopes, courageousness, forgiveness, acceptance, encouragement, etc…) about me. What plan will I make to improve myself and become my child's best example?

_____

_____

_____

_____

TODAY'S DATE _____

CHILD'S NAME/AGE _____

_____

1. What behavior did my child exhibit today that caught my attention?

   _____
   _____

2. Do I want my child to keep it? Is it in my child's greatest interest?

   _____
   _____

3. Did watching that trait make me laugh and smile?

   _____
   _____

4. Did the behavior trigger me? What would I like my child to exhibit instead?

   _____
   _____

TO KNOW THYSELF IS THE BEGINNING OF WISDOM.
SOCRATES

5. Do I even see the behavior in myself? Am I willing to change or alter the same behavior in me?

_____

_____

6. What change do I need to make in myself to be a better role model, so my young one will exhibit **that** behavior instead?

_____

_____

_____

7. Time to take a moment to reflect on what I've learned about myself from my child. Jot down a few thoughts (i.e., wishes, hopes, courageousness, forgiveness, acceptance, encouragement, etc…) about me. What plan will I make to improve myself and become my child's best example?

_____

_____

_____

_____

TODAY'S DATE _____

CHILD'S NAME/AGE _____

_____

1. What behavior did my child exhibit today that caught my attention?

2. Do I want my child to keep it? Is it in my child's greatest interest?

3. Did watching that trait make me laugh and smile?

4. Did the behavior trigger me? What would I like my child to exhibit instead?

> TO KNOW THYSELF IS THE BEGINNING OF WISDOM.
> SOCRATES

5. Do I even see the behavior in myself? Am I willing to change or alter the same behavior in me?

_____

_____

6. What change do I need to make in myself to be a better role model, so my young one will exhibit **that** behavior instead?

_____

_____

7. Time to take a moment to reflect on what I've learned about myself from my child. Jot down a few thoughts (i.e., wishes, hopes, courageousness, forgiveness, acceptance, encouragement, etc...) about me. What plan will I make to improve myself and become my child's best example?

_____

_____

_____

_____

TODAY'S DATE _____
CHILD'S NAME/AGE _____
_____

1. What behavior did my child exhibit today that caught my attention?

   _____
   _____

2. Do I want my child to keep it? Is it in my child's greatest interest?

   _____
   _____

3. Did watching that trait make me laugh and smile?

   _____
   _____

4. Did the behavior trigger me? What would I like my child to exhibit instead?

   _____
   _____

TO KNOW THYSELF IS THE BEGINNING OF WISDOM.
SOCRATES

5. Do I even see the behavior in myself? Am I willing to change or alter the same behavior in me?

6. What change do I need to make in myself to be a better role model, so my young one will exhibit **that** behavior instead?

7. Time to take a moment to reflect on what I've learned about myself from my child. Jot down a few thoughts (i.e., wishes, hopes, courageousness, forgiveness, acceptance, encouragement, etc…) about me. What plan will I make to improve myself and become my child's best example?

TODAY'S DATE _____

CHILD'S NAME/AGE _____

_____

1. What behavior did my child exhibit today that caught my attention?

   _____
   _____

2. Do I want my child to keep it? Is it in my child's greatest interest?

   _____
   _____

3. Did watching that trait make me laugh and smile?

   _____
   _____

4. Did the behavior trigger me? What would I like my child to exhibit instead?

   _____
   _____

TO KNOW THYSELF IS THE BEGINNING OF WISDOM.
SOCRATES

5. Do I even see the behavior in myself? Am I willing to change or alter the same behavior in me?

_____

_____

6. What change do I need to make in myself to be a better role model, so my young one will exhibit **that** behavior instead?

_____

_____

_____

7. Time to take a moment to reflect on what I've learned about myself from my child. Jot down a few thoughts (i.e., wishes, hopes, courageousness, forgiveness, acceptance, encouragement, etc...) about me. What plan will I make to improve myself and become my child's best example?

_____

_____

_____

_____

_____

TODAY'S DATE   _____
CHILD'S NAME/AGE _____
_____

1. What behavior did my child exhibit today that caught my attention?

   _____

   _____

2. Do I want my child to keep it? Is it in my child's greatest interest?

   _____

   _____

3. Did watching that trait make me laugh and smile?

   _____

   _____

4. Did the behavior trigger me? What would I like my child to exhibit instead?

   _____

   _____

TO KNOW THYSELF IS THE BEGINNING OF WISDOM.
SOCRATES

5. Do I even see the behavior in myself? Am I willing to change or alter the same behavior in me?

_____

_____

6. What change do I need to make in myself to be a better role model, so my young one will exhibit **that** behavior instead?

_____

_____

_____

7. Time to take a moment to reflect on what I've learned about myself from my child. Jot down a few thoughts (i.e., wishes, hopes, courageousness, forgiveness, acceptance, encouragement, etc...) about me. What plan will I make to improve myself and become my child's best example?

_____

_____

_____

_____

TODAY'S DATE _____

CHILD'S NAME/AGE _____

_____

1. What behavior did my child exhibit today that caught my attention?

   _____
   _____

2. Do I want my child to keep it? Is it in my child's greatest interest?

   _____
   _____

3. Did watching that trait make me laugh and smile?

   _____
   _____

4. Did the behavior trigger me? What would I like my child to exhibit instead?

   _____
   _____

TO KNOW THYSELF IS THE BEGINNING OF WISDOM.
SOCRATES

5. Do I even see the behavior in myself? Am I willing to change or alter the same behavior in me?

_____

_____

6. What change do I need to make in myself to be a better role model, so my young one will exhibit **that** behavior instead?

_____

_____

_____

7. Time to take a moment to reflect on what I've learned about myself from my child. Jot down a few thoughts (i.e., wishes, hopes, courageousness, forgiveness, acceptance, encouragement, etc...) about me. What plan will I make to improve myself and become my child's best example?

_____

_____

_____

_____

TODAY'S DATE _____

CHILD'S NAME/AGE _____

_____

1. What behavior did my child exhibit today that caught my attention?

   _____

   _____

2. Do I want my child to keep it? Is it in my child's greatest interest?

   _____

   _____

3. Did watching that trait make me laugh and smile?

   _____

   _____

4. Did the behavior trigger me? What would I like my child to exhibit instead?

   _____

   _____

To know thyself is the beginning of wisdom.
Socrates

5. Do I even see the behavior in myself? Am I willing to change or alter the same behavior in me?

_____

_____

6. What change do I need to make in myself to be a better role model, so my young one will exhibit **that** behavior instead?

_____

_____

_____

7. Time to take a moment to reflect on what I've learned about myself from my child. Jot down a few thoughts (i.e., wishes, hopes, courageousness, forgiveness, acceptance, encouragement, etc…) about me. What plan will I make to improve myself and become my child's best example?

_____

_____

_____

_____

TODAY'S DATE _____

CHILD'S NAME/AGE _____

_____

1. What behavior did my child exhibit today that caught my attention?

_____

_____

2. Do I want my child to keep it? Is it in my child's greatest interest?

_____

_____

3. Did watching that trait make me laugh and smile?

_____

_____

4. Did the behavior trigger me? What would I like my child to exhibit instead?

_____

_____

TO KNOW THYSELF IS THE BEGINNING OF WISDOM.
SOCRATES

5. Do I even see the behavior in myself? Am I willing to change or alter the same behavior in me?

6. What change do I need to make in myself to be a better role model, so my young one will exhibit **that** behavior instead?

7. Time to take a moment to reflect on what I've learned about myself from my child. Jot down a few thoughts (i.e., wishes, hopes, courageousness, forgiveness, acceptance, encouragement, etc…) about me. What plan will I make to improve myself and become my child's best example?

TODAY'S DATE _____

CHILD'S NAME/AGE _____

_____

1. What behavior did my child exhibit today that caught my attention?

   _____

   _____

2. Do I want my child to keep it? Is it in my child's greatest interest?

   _____

   _____

3. Did watching that trait make me laugh and smile?

   _____

   _____

4. Did the behavior trigger me? What would I like my child to exhibit instead?

   _____

   _____

To know thyself is the beginning of wisdom.
Socrates

5. Do I even see the behavior in myself? Am I willing to change or alter the same behavior in me?

_____
_____

6. What change do I need to make in myself to be a better role model, so my young one will exhibit **that** behavior instead?

_____
_____
_____

7. Time to take a moment to reflect on what I've learned about myself from my child. Jot down a few thoughts (i.e., wishes, hopes, courageousness, forgiveness, acceptance, encouragement, etc…) about me. What plan will I make to improve myself and become my child's best example?

_____
_____
_____
_____

TODAY'S DATE _____

CHILD'S NAME/AGE _____

_____

1. What behavior did my child exhibit today that caught my attention?

   _____

   _____

2. Do I want my child to keep it? Is it in my child's greatest interest?

   _____

   _____

3. Did watching that trait make me laugh and smile?

   _____

   _____

4. Did the behavior trigger me? What would I like my child to exhibit instead?

   _____

   _____

To know thyself is the beginning of wisdom.

Socrates

5. Do I even see the behavior in myself? Am I willing to change or alter the same behavior in me?

6. What change do I need to make in myself to be a better role model, so my young one will exhibit **that** behavior instead?

7. Time to take a moment to reflect on what I've learned about myself from my child. Jot down a few thoughts (i.e., wishes, hopes, courageousness, forgiveness, acceptance, encouragement, etc...) about me. What plan will I make to improve myself and become my child's best example?

TODAY'S DATE _____

CHILD'S NAME/AGE _____

_____

1. What behavior did my child exhibit today that caught my attention?

_____

_____

2. Do I want my child to keep it? Is it in my child's greatest interest?

_____

_____

3. Did watching that trait make me laugh and smile?

_____

_____

4. Did the behavior trigger me? What would I like my child to exhibit instead?

_____

_____

To know thyself is the beginning of wisdom.
Socrates

5. Do I even see the behavior in myself? Am I willing to change or alter the same behavior in me?

6. What change do I need to make in myself to be a better role model, so my young one will exhibit **that** behavior instead?

7. Time to take a moment to reflect on what I've learned about myself from my child. Jot down a few thoughts (i.e., wishes, hopes, courageousness, forgiveness, acceptance, encouragement, etc…) about me. What plan will I make to improve myself and become my child's best example?

TODAY'S DATE _____

CHILD'S NAME/AGE _____

_____

1. What behavior did my child exhibit today that caught my attention?

   _____
   _____

2. Do I want my child to keep it? Is it in my child's greatest interest?

   _____
   _____

3. Did watching that trait make me laugh and smile?

   _____
   _____

4. Did the behavior trigger me? What would I like my child to exhibit instead?

   _____
   _____

To know thyself is the beginning of wisdom.
Socrates

5. Do I even see the behavior in myself? Am I willing to change or alter the same behavior in me?

_____

_____

6. What change do I need to make in myself to be a better role model, so my young one will exhibit **that** behavior instead?

_____

_____

_____

7. Time to take a moment to reflect on what I've learned about myself from my child. Jot down a few thoughts (i.e., wishes, hopes, courageousness, forgiveness, acceptance, encouragement, etc…) about me. What plan will I make to improve myself and become my child's best example?

_____

_____

_____

_____

TODAY'S DATE _____

CHILD'S NAME/AGE _____

_____

1. What behavior did my child exhibit today that caught my attention?

   _____

   _____

2. Do I want my child to keep it? Is it in my child's greatest interest?

   _____

   _____

3. Did watching that trait make me laugh and smile?

   _____

   _____

4. Did the behavior trigger me? What would I like my child to exhibit instead?

   _____

   _____

TO KNOW THYSELF IS THE BEGINNING OF WISDOM.
SOCRATES

DAILY PARENTING REFLECTIONS

5. Do I even see the behavior in myself? Am I willing to change or alter the same behavior in me?

___

6. What change do I need to make in myself to be a better role model, so my young one will exhibit **that** behavior instead?

___

7. Time to take a moment to reflect on what I've learned about myself from my child. Jot down a few thoughts (i.e., wishes, hopes, courageousness, forgiveness, acceptance, encouragement, etc...) about me. What plan will I make to improve myself and become my child's best example?

___

TODAY'S DATE _____

CHILD'S NAME/AGE _____

_____

1. What behavior did my child exhibit today that caught my attention?

———————————————————————————

———————————————————————————

2. Do I want my child to keep it? Is it in my child's greatest interest?

———————————————————————————

———————————————————————————

3. Did watching that trait make me laugh and smile?

———————————————————————————

———————————————————————————

4. Did the behavior trigger me? What would I like my child to exhibit instead?

———————————————————————————

———————————————————————————

To know thyself is the beginning of wisdom.
Socrates

5. Do I even see the behavior in myself? Am I willing to change or alter the same behavior in me?

_____

_____

6. What change do I need to make in myself to be a better role model, so my young one will exhibit **that** behavior instead?

_____

_____

_____

7. Time to take a moment to reflect on what I've learned about myself from my child. Jot down a few thoughts (i.e., wishes, hopes, courageousness, forgiveness, acceptance, encouragement, etc…) about me. What plan will I make to improve myself and become my child's best example?

_____

_____

_____

_____

TODAY'S DATE _____

CHILD'S NAME/AGE _____

_____

1. What behavior did my child exhibit today that caught my attention?

   _____

   _____

2. Do I want my child to keep it? Is it in my child's greatest interest?

   _____

   _____

3. Did watching that trait make me laugh and smile?

   _____

   _____

4. Did the behavior trigger me? What would I like my child to exhibit instead?

   _____

   _____

TO KNOW THYSELF IS THE BEGINNING OF WISDOM.
SOCRATES

5. Do I even see the behavior in myself? Am I willing to change or alter the same behavior in me?

   _____

   _____

6. What change do I need to make in myself to be a better role model, so my young one will exhibit **that** behavior instead?

   _____

   _____

   _____

7. Time to take a moment to reflect on what I've learned about myself from my child. Jot down a few thoughts (i.e., wishes, hopes, courageousness, forgiveness, acceptance, encouragement, etc…) about me. What plan will I make to improve myself and become my child's best example?

   _____

   _____

   _____

   _____

TODAY'S DATE _____

CHILD'S NAME/AGE _____

_____

1. What behavior did my child exhibit today that caught my attention?

   _____

   _____

2. Do I want my child to keep it? Is it in my child's greatest interest?

   _____

   _____

3. Did watching that trait make me laugh and smile?

   _____

   _____

4. Did the behavior trigger me? What would I like my child to exhibit instead?

   _____

   _____

To know thyself is the beginning of wisdom.
Socrates

5. Do I even see the behavior in myself? Am I willing to change or alter the same behavior in me?

_____
_____

6. What change do I need to make in myself to be a better role model, so my young one will exhibit **that** behavior instead?

_____
_____
_____

7. Time to take a moment to reflect on what I've learned about myself from my child. Jot down a few thoughts (i.e., wishes, hopes, courageousness, forgiveness, acceptance, encouragement, etc…) about me. What plan will I make to improve myself and become my child's best example?

_____
_____
_____
_____

TODAY'S DATE _____

CHILD'S NAME/AGE _____

_____

1. What behavior did my child exhibit today that caught my attention?

   _____
   _____

2. Do I want my child to keep it? Is it in my child's greatest interest?

   _____
   _____

3. Did watching that trait make me laugh and smile?

   _____
   _____

4. Did the behavior trigger me? What would I like my child to exhibit instead?

   _____
   _____

TO KNOW THYSELF IS THE BEGINNING OF WISDOM.
SOCRATES

5. Do I even see the behavior in myself? Am I willing to change or alter the same behavior in me?

_____

_____

6. What change do I need to make in myself to be a better role model, so my young one will exhibit **that** behavior instead?

_____

_____

_____

7. Time to take a moment to reflect on what I've learned about myself from my child. Jot down a few thoughts (i.e., wishes, hopes, courageousness, forgiveness, acceptance, encouragement, etc...) about me. What plan will I make to improve myself and become my child's best example?

_____

_____

_____

_____

TODAY'S DATE _____

CHILD'S NAME/AGE _____

_____

1. What behavior did my child exhibit today that caught my attention?

_____

_____

2. Do I want my child to keep it? Is it in my child's greatest interest?

_____

_____

3. Did watching that trait make me laugh and smile?

_____

_____

4. Did the behavior trigger me? What would I like my child to exhibit instead?

_____

_____

To know thyself is the beginning of wisdom.
Socrates

5. Do I even see the behavior in myself? Am I willing to change or alter the same behavior in me?

6. What change do I need to make in myself to be a better role model, so my young one will exhibit **that** behavior instead?

7. Time to take a moment to reflect on what I've learned about myself from my child. Jot down a few thoughts (i.e., wishes, hopes, courageousness, forgiveness, acceptance, encouragement, etc…) about me. What plan will I make to improve myself and become my child's best example?

TODAY'S DATE _____

CHILD'S NAME/AGE _____

_____

1. What behavior did my child exhibit today that caught my attention?

   _____
   _____

2. Do I want my child to keep it? Is it in my child's greatest interest?

   _____
   _____

3. Did watching that trait make me laugh and smile?

   _____
   _____

4. Did the behavior trigger me? What would I like my child to exhibit instead?

   _____
   _____

TO KNOW THYSELF IS THE BEGINNING OF WISDOM.
SOCRATES

5. Do I even see the behavior in myself? Am I willing to change or alter the same behavior in me?

6. What change do I need to make in myself to be a better role model, so my young one will exhibit **that** behavior instead?

7. Time to take a moment to reflect on what I've learned about myself from my child. Jot down a few thoughts (i.e., wishes, hopes, courageousness, forgiveness, acceptance, encouragement, etc…) about me. What plan will I make to improve myself and become my child's best example?

TODAY'S DATE _____

CHILD'S NAME/AGE _____

_____

1. What behavior did my child exhibit today that caught my attention?

_____

_____

2. Do I want my child to keep it? Is it in my child's greatest interest?

_____

_____

3. Did watching that trait make me laugh and smile?

_____

_____

4. Did the behavior trigger me? What would I like my child to exhibit instead?

_____

_____

To know thyself is the beginning of wisdom.
Socrates

5. Do I even see the behavior in myself? Am I willing to change or alter the same behavior in me?

_____

_____

6. What change do I need to make in myself to be a better role model, so my young one will exhibit **that** behavior instead?

_____

_____

_____

7. Time to take a moment to reflect on what I've learned about myself from my child. Jot down a few thoughts (i.e., wishes, hopes, courageousness, forgiveness, acceptance, encouragement, etc…) about me. What plan will I make to improve myself and become my child's best example?

_____

_____

_____

_____

TODAY'S DATE _____

CHILD'S NAME/AGE _____

_____

1. What behavior did my child exhibit today that caught my attention?

_____

_____

2. Do I want my child to keep it? Is it in my child's greatest interest?

_____

_____

3. Did watching that trait make me laugh and smile?

_____

_____

4. Did the behavior trigger me? What would I like my child to exhibit instead?

_____

_____

To know thyself is the beginning of wisdom.
Socrates

5. Do I even see the behavior in myself? Am I willing to change or alter the same behavior in me?

_____

_____

6. What change do I need to make in myself to be a better role model, so my young one will exhibit **that** behavior instead?

_____

_____

_____

7. Time to take a moment to reflect on what I've learned about myself from my child. Jot down a few thoughts (i.e., wishes, hopes, courageousness, forgiveness, acceptance, encouragement, etc...) about me. What plan will I make to improve myself and become my child's best example?

_____

_____

_____

_____

TODAY'S DATE _____

CHILD'S NAME/AGE _____

_____

1. What behavior did my child exhibit today that caught my attention?

   _____

   _____

2. Do I want my child to keep it? Is it in my child's greatest interest?

   _____

   _____

3. Did watching that trait make me laugh and smile?

   _____

   _____

4. Did the behavior trigger me? What would I like my child to exhibit instead?

   _____

   _____

To know thyself is the beginning of wisdom.

Socrates

5. Do I even see the behavior in myself? Am I willing to change or alter the same behavior in me?

6. What change do I need to make in myself to be a better role model, so my young one will exhibit **that** behavior instead?

7. Time to take a moment to reflect on what I've learned about myself from my child. Jot down a few thoughts (i.e., wishes, hopes, courageousness, forgiveness, acceptance, encouragement, etc...) about me. What plan will I make to improve myself and become my child's best example?

TODAY'S DATE _____

CHILD'S NAME/AGE _____

_____

1. What behavior did my child exhibit today that caught my attention?

   _____

   _____

2. Do I want my child to keep it? Is it in my child's greatest interest?

   _____

   _____

3. Did watching that trait make me laugh and smile?

   _____

   _____

4. Did the behavior trigger me? What would I like my child to exhibit instead?

   _____

   _____

TO KNOW THYSELF IS THE BEGINNING OF WISDOM.
SOCRATES

5. Do I even see the behavior in myself? Am I willing to change or alter the same behavior in me?

_____

_____

6. What change do I need to make in myself to be a better role model, so my young one will exhibit **that** behavior instead?

_____

_____

7. Time to take a moment to reflect on what I've learned about myself from my child. Jot down a few thoughts (i.e., wishes, hopes, courageousness, forgiveness, acceptance, encouragement, etc…) about me. What plan will I make to improve myself and become my child's best example?

_____

_____

_____

_____

TODAY'S DATE _____

CHILD'S NAME/AGE _____

_____

1. What behavior did my child exhibit today that caught my attention?

   _____

   _____

2. Do I want my child to keep it? Is it in my child's greatest interest?

   _____

   _____

3. Did watching that trait make me laugh and smile?

   _____

   _____

4. Did the behavior trigger me? What would I like my child to exhibit instead?

   _____

   _____

To know thyself is the beginning of wisdom.
Socrates

5. Do I even see the behavior in myself? Am I willing to change or alter the same behavior in me?

_____

_____

6. What change do I need to make in myself to be a better role model, so my young one will exhibit **that** behavior instead?

_____

_____

_____

7. Time to take a moment to reflect on what I've learned about myself from my child. Jot down a few thoughts (i.e., wishes, hopes, courageousness, forgiveness, acceptance, encouragement, etc...) about me. What plan will I make to improve myself and become my child's best example?

_____

_____

_____

_____

TODAY'S DATE _____

CHILD'S NAME/AGE _____

_____

1. What behavior did my child exhibit today that caught my attention?

   _____
   _____

2. Do I want my child to keep it? Is it in my child's greatest interest?

   _____
   _____

3. Did watching that trait make me laugh and smile?

   _____
   _____

4. Did the behavior trigger me? What would I like my child to exhibit instead?

   _____
   _____

To know thyself is the beginning of wisdom.
Socrates

5. Do I even see the behavior in myself? Am I willing to change or alter the same behavior in me?

_____
_____

6. What change do I need to make in myself to be a better role model, so my young one will exhibit **that** behavior instead?

_____
_____
_____

7. Time to take a moment to reflect on what I've learned about myself from my child. Jot down a few thoughts (i.e., wishes, hopes, courageousness, forgiveness, acceptance, encouragement, etc…) about me. What plan will I make to improve myself and become my child's best example?

_____
_____
_____
_____

TODAY'S DATE _____

CHILD'S NAME/AGE _____

_____

1. What behavior did my child exhibit today that caught my attention?

   _____

   _____

2. Do I want my child to keep it? Is it in my child's greatest interest?

   _____

   _____

3. Did watching that trait make me laugh and smile?

   _____

   _____

4. Did the behavior trigger me? What would I like my child to exhibit instead?

   _____

   _____

To know thyself is the beginning of wisdom.
Socrates

5. Do I even see the behavior in myself? Am I willing to change or alter the same behavior in me?

_____

_____

6. What change do I need to make in myself to be a better role model, so my young one will exhibit **that** behavior instead?

_____

_____

7. Time to take a moment to reflect on what I've learned about myself from my child. Jot down a few thoughts (i.e., wishes, hopes, courageousness, forgiveness, acceptance, encouragement, etc…) about me. What plan will I make to improve myself and become my child's best example?

_____

_____

_____

_____

TODAY'S DATE _____

CHILD'S NAME/AGE _____

_____

1. What behavior did my child exhibit today that caught my attention?

   _____

   _____

2. Do I want my child to keep it? Is it in my child's greatest interest?

   _____

   _____

3. Did watching that trait make me laugh and smile?

   _____

   _____

4. Did the behavior trigger me? What would I like my child to exhibit instead?

   _____

   _____

TO KNOW THYSELF IS THE BEGINNING OF WISDOM.
SOCRATES

5. Do I even see the behavior in myself? Am I willing to change or alter the same behavior in me?

_____

_____

6. What change do I need to make in myself to be a better role model, so my young one will exhibit **that** behavior instead?

_____

_____

_____

7. Time to take a moment to reflect on what I've learned about myself from my child. Jot down a few thoughts (i.e., wishes, hopes, courageousness, forgiveness, acceptance, encouragement, etc...) about me. What plan will I make to improve myself and become my child's best example?

_____

_____

_____

_____

TODAY'S DATE _____

CHILD'S NAME/AGE _____

_____

1. What behavior did my child exhibit today that caught my attention?

   _____
   _____

2. Do I want my child to keep it? Is it in my child's greatest interest?

   _____
   _____

3. Did watching that trait make me laugh and smile?

   _____
   _____

4. Did the behavior trigger me? What would I like my child to exhibit instead?

   _____
   _____

TO KNOW THYSELF IS THE BEGINNING OF WISDOM.
SOCRATES

5. Do I even see the behavior in myself? Am I willing to change or alter the same behavior in me?

_____

_____

6. What change do I need to make in myself to be a better role model, so my young one will exhibit **that** behavior instead?

_____

_____

_____

7. Time to take a moment to reflect on what I've learned about myself from my child. Jot down a few thoughts (i.e., wishes, hopes, courageousness, forgiveness, acceptance, encouragement, etc…) about me. What plan will I make to improve myself and become my child's best example?

_____

_____

_____

_____

TODAY'S DATE _____

CHILD'S NAME/AGE _____

_____

1. What behavior did my child exhibit today that caught my attention?

_____

_____

2. Do I want my child to keep it? Is it in my child's greatest interest?

_____

_____

3. Did watching that trait make me laugh and smile?

_____

_____

4. Did the behavior trigger me? What would I like my child to exhibit instead?

_____

_____

To know thyself is the beginning of wisdom.
Socrates

5. Do I even see the behavior in myself? Am I willing to change or alter the same behavior in me?

6. What change do I need to make in myself to be a better role model, so my young one will exhibit **that** behavior instead?

7. Time to take a moment to reflect on what I've learned about myself from my child. Jot down a few thoughts (i.e., wishes, hopes, courageousness, forgiveness, acceptance, encouragement, etc…) about me. What plan will I make to improve myself and become my child's best example?

TODAY'S DATE _____

CHILD'S NAME/AGE _____

_____

1. What behavior did my child exhibit today that caught my attention?

   _____

   _____

2. Do I want my child to keep it? Is it in my child's greatest interest?

   _____

   _____

3. Did watching that trait make me laugh and smile?

   _____

   _____

4. Did the behavior trigger me? What would I like my child to exhibit instead?

   _____

   _____

TO KNOW THYSELF IS THE BEGINNING OF WISDOM.
SOCRATES

5. Do I even see the behavior in myself? Am I willing to change or alter the same behavior in me?

_____

_____

6. What change do I need to make in myself to be a better role model, so my young one will exhibit **that** behavior instead?

_____

_____

_____

7. Time to take a moment to reflect on what I've learned about myself from my child. Jot down a few thoughts (i.e., wishes, hopes, courageousness, forgiveness, acceptance, encouragement, etc…) about me. What plan will I make to improve myself and become my child's best example?

_____

_____

_____

_____

TODAY'S DATE _____

CHILD'S NAME/AGE _____

_____

1. What behavior did my child exhibit today that caught my attention?

   _____

   _____

2. Do I want my child to keep it? Is it in my child's greatest interest?

   _____

   _____

3. Did watching that trait make me laugh and smile?

   _____

   _____

4. Did the behavior trigger me? What would I like my child to exhibit instead?

   _____

   _____

To know thyself is the beginning of wisdom.
Socrates

5. Do I even see the behavior in myself? Am I willing to change or alter the same behavior in me?

6. What change do I need to make in myself to be a better role model, so my young one will exhibit **that** behavior instead?

7. Time to take a moment to reflect on what I've learned about myself from my child. Jot down a few thoughts (i.e., wishes, hopes, courageousness, forgiveness, acceptance, encouragement, etc…) about me. What plan will I make to improve myself and become my child's best example?

TODAY'S DATE _____

CHILD'S NAME/AGE _____

_____

1. What behavior did my child exhibit today that caught my attention?

   _____
   _____

2. Do I want my child to keep it? Is it in my child's greatest interest?

   _____
   _____

3. Did watching that trait make me laugh and smile?

   _____
   _____

4. Did the behavior trigger me? What would I like my child to exhibit instead?

   _____
   _____

To know thyself is the beginning of wisdom.
Socrates

5. Do I even see the behavior in myself? Am I willing to change or alter the same behavior in me?

_____

_____

6. What change do I need to make in myself to be a better role model, so my young one will exhibit **that** behavior instead?

_____

_____

_____

7. Time to take a moment to reflect on what I've learned about myself from my child. Jot down a few thoughts (i.e., wishes, hopes, courageousness, forgiveness, acceptance, encouragement, etc…) about me. What plan will I make to improve myself and become my child's best example?

_____

_____

_____

_____

TODAY'S DATE _____

CHILD'S NAME/AGE _____

_____

1. What behavior did my child exhibit today that caught my attention?

   _____
   _____

2. Do I want my child to keep it? Is it in my child's greatest interest?

   _____
   _____

3. Did watching that trait make me laugh and smile?

   _____
   _____

4. Did the behavior trigger me? What would I like my child to exhibit instead?

   _____
   _____

To know thyself is the beginning of wisdom.
Socrates

5. Do I even see the behavior in myself? Am I willing to change or alter the same behavior in me?

6. What change do I need to make in myself to be a better role model, so my young one will exhibit **that** behavior instead?

7. Time to take a moment to reflect on what I've learned about myself from my child. Jot down a few thoughts (i.e., wishes, hopes, courageousness, forgiveness, acceptance, encouragement, etc…) about me. What plan will I make to improve myself and become my child's best example?

TODAY'S DATE _____

CHILD'S NAME/AGE _____

_____

1. What behavior did my child exhibit today that caught my attention?

   _____

   _____

2. Do I want my child to keep it? Is it in my child's greatest interest?

   _____

   _____

3. Did watching that trait make me laugh and smile?

   _____

   _____

4. Did the behavior trigger me? What would I like my child to exhibit instead?

   _____

   _____

To know thyself is the beginning of wisdom.
Socrates

5. Do I even see the behavior in myself? Am I willing to change or alter the same behavior in me?

_____

_____

6. What change do I need to make in myself to be a better role model, so my young one will exhibit **that** behavior instead?

_____

_____

_____

7. Time to take a moment to reflect on what I've learned about myself from my child. Jot down a few thoughts (i.e., wishes, hopes, courageousness, forgiveness, acceptance, encouragement, etc…) about me. What plan will I make to improve myself and become my child's best example?

_____

_____

_____

_____

TODAY'S DATE _____

CHILD'S NAME/AGE _____

_____

1. What behavior did my child exhibit today that caught my attention?

_____

_____

2. Do I want my child to keep it? Is it in my child's greatest interest?

_____

_____

3. Did watching that trait make me laugh and smile?

_____

_____

4. Did the behavior trigger me? What would I like my child to exhibit instead?

_____

_____

To know thyself is the beginning of wisdom.
Socrates

5. Do I even see the behavior in myself? Am I willing to change or alter the same behavior in me?

6. What change do I need to make in myself to be a better role model, so my young one will exhibit **that** behavior instead?

7. Time to take a moment to reflect on what I've learned about myself from my child. Jot down a few thoughts (i.è., wishes, hopes, courageousness, forgiveness, acceptance, encouragement, etc...) about me. What plan will I make to improve myself and become my child's best example?

TODAY'S DATE _____

CHILD'S NAME/AGE _____

_____

1. What behavior did my child exhibit today that caught my attention?

   _____

   _____

2. Do I want my child to keep it? Is it in my child's greatest interest?

   _____

   _____

3. Did watching that trait make me laugh and smile?

   _____

   _____

4. Did the behavior trigger me? What would I like my child to exhibit instead?

   _____

   _____

To know thyself is the beginning of wisdom.

Socrates

5. Do I even see the behavior in myself? Am I willing to change or alter the same behavior in me?

6. What change do I need to make in myself to be a better role model, so my young one will exhibit **that** behavior instead?

7. Time to take a moment to reflect on what I've learned about myself from my child. Jot down a few thoughts (i.e., wishes, hopes, courageousness, forgiveness, acceptance, encouragement, etc…) about me. What plan will I make to improve myself and become my child's best example?

TODAY'S DATE _____

CHILD'S NAME/AGE _____

_____

1. What behavior did my child exhibit today that caught my attention?

   _____

   _____

2. Do I want my child to keep it? Is it in my child's greatest interest?

   _____

   _____

3. Did watching that trait make me laugh and smile?

   _____

   _____

4. Did the behavior trigger me? What would I like my child to exhibit instead?

   _____

   _____

To know thyself is the beginning of wisdom.
Socrates

5. Do I even see the behavior in myself? Am I willing to change or alter the same behavior in me?

_____

_____

6. What change do I need to make in myself to be a better role model, so my young one will exhibit **that** behavior instead?

_____

_____

_____

7. Time to take a moment to reflect on what I've learned about myself from my child. Jot down a few thoughts (i.e., wishes, hopes, courageousness, forgiveness, acceptance, encouragement, etc…) about me. What plan will I make to improve myself and become my child's best example?

_____

_____

_____

_____

TODAY'S DATE _____

CHILD'S NAME/AGE _____

_____

1. What behavior did my child exhibit today that caught my attention?

   _____
   _____

2. Do I want my child to keep it? Is it in my child's greatest interest?

   _____
   _____

3. Did watching that trait make me laugh and smile?

   _____
   _____

4. Did the behavior trigger me? What would I like my child to exhibit instead?

   _____
   _____

TO KNOW THYSELF IS THE BEGINNING OF WISDOM.
SOCRATES

5. Do I even see the behavior in myself? Am I willing to change or alter the same behavior in me?

6. What change do I need to make in myself to be a better role model, so my young one will exhibit **that** behavior instead?

7. Time to take a moment to reflect on what I've learned about myself from my child. Jot down a few thoughts (i.e., wishes, hopes, courageousness, forgiveness, acceptance, encouragement, etc…) about me. What plan will I make to improve myself and become my child's best example?

TODAY'S DATE _____

CHILD'S NAME/AGE _____

_____

1. What behavior did my child exhibit today that caught my attention?

_____

_____

2. Do I want my child to keep it? Is it in my child's greatest interest?

_____

_____

3. Did watching that trait make me laugh and smile?

_____

_____

4. Did the behavior trigger me? What would I like my child to exhibit instead?

_____

_____

TO KNOW THYSELF IS THE BEGINNING OF WISDOM.
SOCRATES

5. Do I even see the behavior in myself? Am I willing to change or alter the same behavior in me?

6. What change do I need to make in myself to be a better role model, so my young one will exhibit **that** behavior instead?

7. Time to take a moment to reflect on what I've learned about myself from my child. Jot down a few thoughts (i.e., wishes, hopes, courageousness, forgiveness, acceptance, encouragement, etc...) about me. What plan will I make to improve myself and become my child's best example?

TODAY'S DATE _____

CHILD'S NAME/AGE _____

_____

1. What behavior did my child exhibit today that caught my attention?

   _____
   _____

2. Do I want my child to keep it? Is it in my child's greatest interest?

   _____
   _____

3. Did watching that trait make me laugh and smile?

   _____
   _____

4. Did the behavior trigger me? What would I like my child to exhibit instead?

   _____
   _____

To know thyself is the beginning of wisdom.
Socrates

5. Do I even see the behavior in myself? Am I willing to change or alter the same behavior in me?

6. What change do I need to make in myself to be a better role model, so my young one will exhibit **that** behavior instead?

7. Time to take a moment to reflect on what I've learned about myself from my child. Jot down a few thoughts (i.e., wishes, hopes, courageousness, forgiveness, acceptance, encouragement, etc...) about me. What plan will I make to improve myself and become my child's best example?

TODAY'S DATE _____

CHILD'S NAME/AGE _____

_____

1. What behavior did my child exhibit today that caught my attention?

   _____

   _____

2. Do I want my child to keep it? Is it in my child's greatest interest?

   _____

   _____

3. Did watching that trait make me laugh and smile?

   _____

   _____

4. Did the behavior trigger me? What would I like my child to exhibit instead?

   _____

   _____

TO KNOW THYSELF IS THE BEGINNING OF WISDOM.
SOCRATES

5. Do I even see the behavior in myself? Am I willing to change or alter the same behavior in me?

6. What change do I need to make in myself to be a better role model, so my young one will exhibit **that** behavior instead?

7. Time to take a moment to reflect on what I've learned about myself from my child. Jot down a few thoughts (i.e., wishes, hopes, courageousness, forgiveness, acceptance, encouragement, etc…) about me. What plan will I make to improve myself and become my child's best example?

TODAY'S DATE _____

CHILD'S NAME/AGE _____

_____

1. What behavior did my child exhibit today that caught my attention?

   _____
   _____

2. Do I want my child to keep it? Is it in my child's greatest interest?

   _____
   _____

3. Did watching that trait make me laugh and smile?

   _____
   _____

4. Did the behavior trigger me? What would I like my child to exhibit instead?

   _____
   _____

TO KNOW THYSELF IS THE BEGINNING OF WISDOM.
SOCRATES

5. Do I even see the behavior in myself? Am I willing to change or alter the same behavior in me?

_____

_____

6. What change do I need to make in myself to be a better role model, so my young one will exhibit **that** behavior instead?

_____

_____

_____

7. Time to take a moment to reflect on what I've learned about myself from my child. Jot down a few thoughts (i.e., wishes, hopes, courageousness, forgiveness, acceptance, encouragement, etc…) about me. What plan will I make to improve myself and become my child's best example?

_____

_____

_____

_____

TODAY'S DATE _____

CHILD'S NAME/AGE _____

_____

1. What behavior did my child exhibit today that caught my attention?

   _____

   _____

2. Do I want my child to keep it? Is it in my child's greatest interest?

   _____

   _____

3. Did watching that trait make me laugh and smile?

   _____

   _____

4. Did the behavior trigger me? What would I like my child to exhibit instead?

   _____

   _____

To know thyself is the beginning of wisdom.
Socrates

5. Do I even see the behavior in myself? Am I willing to change or alter the same behavior in me?

_____

_____

6. What change do I need to make in myself to be a better role model, so my young one will exhibit **that** behavior instead?

_____

_____

7. Time to take a moment to reflect on what I've learned about myself from my child. Jot down a few thoughts (i.e., wishes, hopes, courageousness, forgiveness, acceptance, encouragement, etc…) about me. What plan will I make to improve myself and become my child's best example?

_____

_____

_____

_____

TODAY'S DATE _____

CHILD'S NAME/AGE _____

_____

1. What behavior did my child exhibit today that caught my attention?

   _____
   _____

2. Do I want my child to keep it? Is it in my child's greatest interest?

   _____
   _____

3. Did watching that trait make me laugh and smile?

   _____
   _____

4. Did the behavior trigger me? What would I like my child to exhibit instead?

   _____
   _____

To know thyself is the beginning of wisdom.
Socrates

5. Do I even see the behavior in myself? Am I willing to change or alter the same behavior in me?

_____

_____

6. What change do I need to make in myself to be a better role model, so my young one will exhibit **that** behavior instead?

_____

_____

_____

7. Time to take a moment to reflect on what I've learned about myself from my child. Jot down a few thoughts (i.e., wishes, hopes, courageousness, forgiveness, acceptance, encouragement, etc…) about me. What plan will I make to improve myself and become my child's best example?

_____

_____

_____

_____

TODAY'S DATE _____

CHILD'S NAME/AGE _____

_____

1. What behavior did my child exhibit today that caught my attention?

   _____

   _____

2. Do I want my child to keep it? Is it in my child's greatest interest?

   _____

   _____

3. Did watching that trait make me laugh and smile?

   _____

   _____

4. Did the behavior trigger me? What would I like my child to exhibit instead?

   _____

   _____

To know thyself is the beginning of wisdom.
Socrates

5. Do I even see the behavior in myself? Am I willing to change or alter the same behavior in me?

6. What change do I need to make in myself to be a better role model, so my young one will exhibit **that** behavior instead?

7. Time to take a moment to reflect on what I've learned about myself from my child. Jot down a few thoughts (i.e., wishes, hopes, courageousness, forgiveness, acceptance, encouragement, etc…) about me. What plan will I make to improve myself and become my child's best example?

TODAY'S DATE _____

CHILD'S NAME/AGE _____

_____

1. What behavior did my child exhibit today that caught my attention?

___

___

2. Do I want my child to keep it? Is it in my child's greatest interest?

___

___

3. Did watching that trait make me laugh and smile?

___

___

4. Did the behavior trigger me? What would I like my child to exhibit instead?

___

___

TO KNOW THYSELF IS THE BEGINNING OF WISDOM.
SOCRATES

5. Do I even see the behavior in myself? Am I willing to change or alter the same behavior in me?

_____

_____

6. What change do I need to make in myself to be a better role model, so my young one will exhibit **that** behavior instead?

_____

_____

_____

7. Time to take a moment to reflect on what I've learned about myself from my child. Jot down a few thoughts (i.e., wishes, hopes, courageousness, forgiveness, acceptance, encouragement, etc...) about me. What plan will I make to improve myself and become my child's best example?

_____

_____

_____

_____

TODAY'S DATE _____

CHILD'S NAME/AGE _____

_____

1. What behavior did my child exhibit today that caught my attention?

   _____

   _____

2. Do I want my child to keep it? Is it in my child's greatest interest?

   _____

   _____

3. Did watching that trait make me laugh and smile?

   _____

   _____

4. Did the behavior trigger me? What would I like my child to exhibit instead?

   _____

   _____

To know thyself is the beginning of wisdom.
Socrates

5. Do I even see the behavior in myself? Am I willing to change or alter the same behavior in me?

6. What change do I need to make in myself to be a better role model, so my young one will exhibit **that** behavior instead?

7. Time to take a moment to reflect on what I've learned about myself from my child. Jot down a few thoughts (i.e., wishes, hopes, courageousness, forgiveness, acceptance, encouragement, etc…) about me. What plan will I make to improve myself and become my child's best example?

TODAY'S DATE _____

CHILD'S NAME/AGE _____

_____

1. What behavior did my child exhibit today that caught my attention?

   _____

   _____

2. Do I want my child to keep it? Is it in my child's greatest interest?

   _____

   _____

3. Did watching that trait make me laugh and smile?

   _____

   _____

4. Did the behavior trigger me? What would I like my child to exhibit instead?

   _____

   _____

TO KNOW THYSELF IS THE BEGINNING OF WISDOM.
SOCRATES

5. Do I even see the behavior in myself? Am I willing to change or alter the same behavior in me?

___

___

6. What change do I need to make in myself to be a better role model, so my young one will exhibit **that** behavior instead?

___

___

7. Time to take a moment to reflect on what I've learned about myself from my child. Jot down a few thoughts (i.e., wishes, hopes, courageousness, forgiveness, acceptance, encouragement, etc...) about me. What plan will I make to improve myself and become my child's best example?

___

___

___

___

TODAY'S DATE _____

CHILD'S NAME/AGE _____

_____

1. What behavior did my child exhibit today that caught my attention?

   _____

   _____

2. Do I want my child to keep it? Is it in my child's greatest interest?

   _____

   _____

3. Did watching that trait make me laugh and smile?

   _____

   _____

4. Did the behavior trigger me? What would I like my child to exhibit instead?

   _____

   _____

To know thyself is the beginning of wisdom.

Socrates

5. Do I even see the behavior in myself? Am I willing to change or alter the same behavior in me?

_____

_____

6. What change do I need to make in myself to be a better role model, so my young one will exhibit **that** behavior instead?

_____

_____

_____

7. Time to take a moment to reflect on what I've learned about myself from my child. Jot down a few thoughts (i.e., wishes, hopes, courageousness, forgiveness, acceptance, encouragement, etc...) about me. What plan will I make to improve myself and become my child's best example?

_____

_____

_____

_____

TODAY'S DATE _____

CHILD'S NAME/AGE _____

_____

1. What behavior did my child exhibit today that caught my attention?

   _____

   _____

2. Do I want my child to keep it? Is it in my child's greatest interest?

   _____

   _____

3. Did watching that trait make me laugh and smile?

   _____

   _____

4. Did the behavior trigger me? What would I like my child to exhibit instead?

   _____

   _____

To know thyself is the beginning of wisdom.
Socrates

5. Do I even see the behavior in myself? Am I willing to change or alter the same behavior in me?

6. What change do I need to make in myself to be a better role model, so my young one will exhibit **that** behavior instead?

7. Time to take a moment to reflect on what I've learned about myself from my child. Jot down a few thoughts (i.e., wishes, hopes, courageousness, forgiveness, acceptance, encouragement, etc…) about me. What plan will I make to improve myself and become my child's best example?

TODAY'S DATE _____

CHILD'S NAME/AGE _____

_____

1. What behavior did my child exhibit today that caught my attention?

   _____

   _____

2. Do I want my child to keep it? Is it in my child's greatest interest?

   _____

   _____

3. Did watching that trait make me laugh and smile?

   _____

   _____

4. Did the behavior trigger me? What would I like my child to exhibit instead?

   _____

   _____

To know thyself is the beginning of wisdom.
Socrates

5. Do I even see the behavior in myself? Am I willing to change or alter the same behavior in me?

6. What change do I need to make in myself to be a better role model, so my young one will exhibit **that** behavior instead?

7. Time to take a moment to reflect on what I've learned about myself from my child. Jot down a few thoughts (i.e., wishes, hopes, courageousness, forgiveness, acceptance, encouragement, etc…) about me. What plan will I make to improve myself and become my child's best example?

TODAY'S DATE _____

CHILD'S NAME/AGE _____

_____

1. What behavior did my child exhibit today that caught my attention?

_____

_____

2. Do I want my child to keep it? Is it in my child's greatest interest?

_____

_____

3. Did watching that trait make me laugh and smile?

_____

_____

4. Did the behavior trigger me? What would I like my child to exhibit instead?

_____

_____

To know thyself is the beginning of wisdom.
Socrates

5. Do I even see the behavior in myself? Am I willing to change or alter the same behavior in me?

_____
_____

6. What change do I need to make in myself to be a better role model, so my young one will exhibit **that** behavior instead?

_____
_____
_____

7. Time to take a moment to reflect on what I've learned about myself from my child. Jot down a few thoughts (i.e., wishes, hopes, courageousness, forgiveness, acceptance, encouragement, etc…) about me. What plan will I make to improve myself and become my child's best example?

_____
_____
_____
_____
_____

TODAY'S DATE _____

CHILD'S NAME/AGE _____

_____

1. What behavior did my child exhibit today that caught my attention?

   _____

   _____

2. Do I want my child to keep it? Is it in my child's greatest interest?

   _____

   _____

3. Did watching that trait make me laugh and smile?

   _____

   _____

4. Did the behavior trigger me? What would I like my child to exhibit instead?

   _____

   _____

TO KNOW THYSELF IS THE BEGINNING OF WISDOM.

SOCRATES

5. Do I even see the behavior in myself? Am I willing to change or alter the same behavior in me?

6. What change do I need to make in myself to be a better role model, so my young one will exhibit **that** behavior instead?

7. Time to take a moment to reflect on what I've learned about myself from my child. Jot down a few thoughts (i.e., wishes, hopes, courageousness, forgiveness, acceptance, encouragement, etc...) about me. What plan will I make to improve myself and become my child's best example?

TODAY'S DATE _____

CHILD'S NAME/AGE _____

_____

1. What behavior did my child exhibit today that caught my attention?

   _____
   _____

2. Do I want my child to keep it? Is it in my child's greatest interest?

   _____
   _____

3. Did watching that trait make me laugh and smile?

   _____
   _____

4. Did the behavior trigger me? What would I like my child to exhibit instead?

   _____
   _____

To know thyself is the beginning of wisdom.
Socrates

5. Do I even see the behavior in myself? Am I willing to change or alter the same behavior in me?

6. What change do I need to make in myself to be a better role model, so my young one will exhibit **that** behavior instead?

7. Time to take a moment to reflect on what I've learned about myself from my child. Jot down a few thoughts (i.e., wishes, hopes, courageousness, forgiveness, acceptance, encouragement, etc…) about me. What plan will I make to improve myself and become my child's best example?

TODAY'S DATE _____

CHILD'S NAME/AGE _____

_____

1. What behavior did my child exhibit today that caught my attention?

   _____

   _____

2. Do I want my child to keep it? Is it in my child's greatest interest?

   _____

   _____

3. Did watching that trait make me laugh and smile?

   _____

   _____

4. Did the behavior trigger me? What would I like my child to exhibit instead?

   _____

   _____

To know thyself is the beginning of wisdom.
Socrates

5. Do I even see the behavior in myself? Am I willing to change or alter the same behavior in me?

_____

_____

6. What change do I need to make in myself to be a better role model, so my young one will exhibit **that** behavior instead?

_____

_____

_____

7. Time to take a moment to reflect on what I've learned about myself from my child. Jot down a few thoughts (i.e., wishes, hopes, courageousness, forgiveness, acceptance, encouragement, etc…) about me. What plan will I make to improve myself and become my child's best example?

_____

_____

_____

_____

ABOUT THE AUTHOR

R. Jill Maxwell, the author of two romantic suspense fiction novels, **G.A.S.P.** and **B.A.I.T.**, has been weaving stories since childhood. Married for 36 years, she is a proud parent to three young adults and one groovy grandchild. ***Daily Parenting Reflections: A Journey Within*** marks her first venture into non-fiction.

Made in the USA
Las Vegas, NV
03 March 2025